Felix Publishing 2021
email: info.felixpublishing@gmail.com
Print copies available from publisher.

A Pocketbook for Surviving Teaching and Instructing

Print Edition: ISBN: 978-1-925662-38-2
Digital book release: ISBN: 978-1-925662-39-9

Also, in the same series:

A Pocketbook for Hiking and Survival

Author: Dr. Peter T. Scott
Illustrations by the author (my apologies to art)

 Registration:
Thorpe-Bowker +61 3 8517 8342
email: bowkerlink@thorpe.com.au

A Pocketbook for
Surviving
Teaching & Instruction

Dr. Peter T. Scott

FELIX
PUBLISHING

Table of Contents

Chapter One

In the Beginning…

1.1 The aim of this book

This is NOT an academic textbook about Education; rather it is, as the title suggests, a survival guide for those game enough to step in front of an audience and attempt to pass on new information.

There are a great variety of teacher training programs at universities and colleges as well as short-term training courses for instructors, both at the college level or within the particular industry where one would be instructing. This book is meant to complement teacher and instructor training courses as well as to add value to those practitioners who may like to add to their own training and experience. I have always had the attitude that good teachers should also be good learners and always strive to improve their own knowledge and skills. If the reader finds a few useful items in this book then its writing has been justified.

The aim of this book, then is to provide a concise outline of some of the many aspects of teaching and instruction which may be useful for those starting their career, for those who want to value add to their existing knowledge and skills and perhaps also to those who now find themselves in a small-scale teaching situation such as home-schooling.

By the end of the reading of this book, one should be able to:

- list, describe and discuss some of the desirable attributes of a good teacher;

- develop good strategies for preparing and planning lessons using sound educational objectives;

- understand the basics of communications and practice good questioning technique;

- review some of the basic teaching strategies;

- describe some important theories of education which lead to good practice;

- use teaching aids, including the use of sketching, more effectively as part of a planned lesson; and

- develop a sound framework for discipline in the classroom.

I hope that the reader will not find this book too boring, as many books in this subject area often tend to get bogged down with 'academia'. Not hard to do and of course there is a time and place for such books. Many teachers go on to do additional academic programs to add to their expertise and qualifications and this is a good thing. Universities and colleges are places which have the staff, time frame and opportunities where the latest research in education and learning can be undertaken.

1.2 Personal confessions

As an example, perhaps I should get a little personal here, as my reason for writing this book in retirement is to pass on what I have learnt by training and experience over a lifetime (it seems like several!) of study, teaching and instruction. Retirement has several advantages; one of which is to have the time to reflect on a long career and put some of the information gathered down. I do miss the classroom interaction however, but certainly not the problems of administration and dealing with the few obnoxious personalities one finds on rare occasions.

I was lucky; if one can use such a term when one has little choice in one's educational pathway. I grew up in a fairly stable but tough suburb in the southern part of Sydney, Australia and went to the local Primary School. This was a school typical of the age, single gender, comprehensive curriculum with emphasis on the three R's and certainly teacher-centred. Any deviation from the expected code of silent behaviour would most likely end in at least 'two of the best!' As a chronic talker full of curiosity and enthusiasm, it was a good day when I did not get the cane.

At the end of Primary Education, all students sat for a Performance Exam of some sorts resembling many IQ tests. This was to determine the Secondary School and the type of program one was to follow in the future. In the 1950's the government of the day were very oriented towards skills training and so young students had their career pathways predetermined to a certain extent. Most of my school friends from the Primary School were determined to be more suitable for the trades and so were sent to the local Technical High School which gave a three-year terminating program and was about 20 metres from my front door. My results suggested that I should be a 'two-language commercial' type and so I was allocated to a

Selective High School which had a comprehensive curriculum over five years with the view that I would go on to a business college or university at the end. My school was about five kilometres away in the next suburb. Parents who had considerable money and wanted their children to enter the professions could send them to a Private School based on the traditional English grammar school and pay big fees. Universities were very expensive and students whose parents were not rich had to compete for the few Commonwealth or Industry Scholarships available.

I had always wanted to be a teacher from the day I first stepped into my Infants School at age four. I liked the environment and thought it would be a good thing to teach other children about all sorts of things. So, not having any aspirations for university, as no one in my extended family had ever stayed in a school past the age of fifteen, nor was there any money about, I applied for a Teachers' Scholarship.

Fate was generous here and I was offered a scholarship to do a two-year course in Junior Secondary Science Teaching. This was a new and very comprehensive program of study generally five days a week from nine until four or five in the afternoon. We were trained in all of the sciences, including Biology and Geology, which were never offered to boys in High School, as well as Mathematics, Sports (including dancing), Art, English Language, English Literature, Speech, Teaching Method, Child Psychology and of course, Education Theory. There were also at least two Practice Teaching sessions per year when we were released into some poor school to wreak havoc onto their students in the guise of attempting to teach. I survived all of this, graduated and was sent to my first teaching post to do country service in a remote and culturally-barren place called Canberra: the Nation's purpose-built capital. Still a frontier territory (the Australian Capital territory – the ACT), Canberra still relied on the surrounding state of New South Wales to provide its Education system and its teachers.

Having just turned nineteen and clutching the new Junior Science textbook and full of enthusiasm, I arrived at my first school. Well, part of it; as it was still being constructed! The new staff consisted of both permanent and casual staff, and as the only permanently-appointed Science Teacher, I was given instant but unpaid promotion to Acting Head of Science with the task of filling the laboratories with equipment and teaching resources. I had a staff of two and then the next year, of four with laboratories for each teacher. My staff all had university degrees and were generally older than I. In the third year, a permanent Head of Science arrived and I was able get on with just teaching. It was a happy school, well-run and I never forgotten the Headmaster's policies and his assistance in handling students. The HOD (Science) became a long-term friend and his eccentricities became a great model for my later administrative career.

Returning to Sydney to teach in what was termed a challenging school, I discovered what it was like to teach students who generally did not want to be there and who had already started on their career pathways of petty crime. There was also considerable pressure from my superiors to study university part-time. I originally had no aspirations in this area, but succumbed to pressure and enrolled in the seven-year program at the local university. My life then became teaching and surviving during the day, attending lectures at night, a few hours' sleep and then starting over again the next day. Weekends were set aside for assignments and study and the holidays were needed for recovery, university excursions and examinations with more study. So, tell me, why do you want to become a teacher?

1.3 Why become a teacher?

It has been said 'that you don't have to be crazy to be a teacher...but it certainly helps!' People become teachers for many and varied reasons. Over the years I have heard many of these, such as:

a) **they always wanted to become a teacher because they liked to help young people learn and develop.** This is the altruistic reason for becoming a teacher. I guess that this best sums up my reason for joining the profession and I have never regretted it. This should be the main reason why anyone should become a teacher. Any other benefits are a bonus and the disadvantages can be tolerated.

b) **because they come from a family of teachers.** This may further cement family ties but is probably not a good personal reason unless one finds that the enthusiasm of their parents or siblings is also theirs as well. Sometimes having more than one teacher in the family may be too daunting for young children who feel like they are simply in an extended version of the classroom at home. My wife was also a teacher and both my children wisely avoided the teaching profession.

c) **it looked easy and they did not know what else to do.** This seems to be an approach of many young people who get to their final year of High School, or even at the end of a comprehensive university degree and still have no sense of a future career. The ease that they remember is probably connected with the enjoyment they had at doing very little and drifting through their school and university days. Practice Teaching during the early days of their teacher training soon shows that the profession is not for the drifters and people who think teaching is easy. A few dropouts occur here or even worse, some persevere and go on to become bad teachers who do the minimum work possible and achieve a high rate of student dissatisfaction. A few wake up and then have to put in a considerable extra effort to become good teachers.

d) **the pay is good.** Well, it is adequate, and compared to some lowly-paid occupations it may be considered good. Compared to other professions requiring a university degree and at least an extra year of training plus a probationary period, it seems only average. Of course, this varies from the type and level of the teacher and so the starting salary and the maximum salary at that level are the best indicators to look at. Salaries also vary from country to country and also within countries depending upon the government authority, school board and sometimes even with a school, especially independent schools. The media often makes references to teacher bonuses to reward the better teachers but often these fall down when it comes to the criteria used and who makes the final choices. Promotion also often does not mean that the teacher promoted is suited for the next level nor that the assessment process is unbiased. In many systems, male and female teachers share the same pay scale but sometimes there may be inequality one way or another when it comes to bonuses or promotion. Also, the pay rate often drops off rapidly with age so that an attractive initial salary does not suggest that it will keep pace over years, nor are there pay incentives for teachers who go on and do additional training. For example, in my last school with two Masters Degrees and a Doctorate, my salary was identical to other Heads of Department with a basic degree and perhaps some teacher training.

A general viewpoint from the Australian perspective can be found at the website:
https://www.sbs.com.au/news/insight/here-s-what-a-teacher-s-pay-really-looks-like

A good comparison of data for teacher salaries around the world can be found at the OECD website at:
https://data.oecd.org/eduresource/teachers-salaries.htm

Another useful site compares teachers' salaries with other professions at:
https://teachertaskforce.org/sites/default/files/migrate_default_content_files/teachers%20salaries%20in%20comparison%20with%20other%20occupational%20groups_1.pdf
(Printed book readers should type in the first section of the URL and follow links to the file)

e) **the hours and holidays are good.** Well, yes and no. Some of the general public who can only remember back to their unfortunate school days, firmly believe that teachers only work (perhaps) from 9 am until 3 pm and have over six weeks of holidays. Fair enough! I have met a few teachers who should not be in the profession who attempt to aspire to these hours of service and then moan about any extra time that the school may require. Most teachers work well past these hours. Try dating a Primary School teacher and see if you can get a night free!

Most conscientious teachers have extra duties other than the face-to-face classroom time given credit by the unknowing public. As if that isn't enough in some tough schools there are other duties.

Some of the hidden duties include: roll-keeping and student records; pastoral care; playground duty before and after school; parent interviews and general enquiries (if the school lets you have a telephone and teachers are crazy if they give out their personal number); marking homework, assignments and test papers; cleaning out the classroom after lessons over and above where the usual cleaners don't go; conferring with other staff; staff meetings; school in-service courses (usually in the last week of holidays); external conferences; open nights; student clubs; sports events on weekends; sports training; weekend excursions;

military cadets and other youth training schemes and many more impromptu events which seem to suddenly occur. This all assumes that the teacher is NOT doing further private study to enhance their career or to qualify to train students in sports, environmental activities or outdoor education.

Government Education Ministers or School Boards seem to have a genius for deciding on a new education campaign 'demanded' by the public to introduce into schools. These often are shoved into an already-bursting classroom curriculum or added on to the after-school program. These may include 'learn-to-swim', 'driver education', 'multi-culturalism', 'indigenous studies' and so on. All of these are good and valuable for the student's development and time is usually found for them, but it does require extra time for training, preparation and execution. Students also often have to find the time for these activities and are also generally over-worked.

Private (Independent) schools tend to demand more time than government schools, but this also can vary depending upon the school's culture. Private schools often have a strong, inclusive culture in which staff are expected to participate in the overall school life and coach and train teams, supervise weekend sports, run clubs and take on pastoral care duties such as looking after boarding students. This can also occur in government schools. Several of the government schools in which I taught were true 'community schools'; great support came from educationally-minded parents; highly motivated students; and an excellent school administration. Most teachers worked from about 8 am until well after many of the students had left but many did not. There often were after-school sporting activities, clubs, and student work sessions supervised in laboratories, technical workshops, gymnasiums and the library. Many of the students often played in local sporting teams on the weekends and were often supported by staff and fellow students. In one school, the entire State Representative Hockey team consisted of the school's players. Outstanding!

I also worked in government schools where the 9 to 3 rule was applied with a passion. Heaven help any student who walked through the staff carpark at five after three! It was like a Le Mons racing start on steroids! Any after-school demands by the Principal was subject to Union scrutiny! These were not pleasant schools to work in and hopefully now in the receding minority.

Then there are the 'excessive' holidays. True, these are a major plus for the profession, especially if one has a school-age family and can be flexible in taking the wife and children away on a holiday. This of course, works well if both parents are teachers or one parent doesn't work and if the students do not have holiday camps, training and sporting commitments. School holidays are also the most expensive and congested times to travel.

Teachers also often have school holiday commitments other than recovering from the last dreadful Term such as preparing lessons and whole programs for the next Term, supervision of school-sponsored camps, excursions and even overseas visits and so on. The shorter school holidays can often be completely taken up with such activities and if one is lucky, there is usually enough flexibility to get away for some family time during the longer vacations.

Some interesting web pages on this topic can be found at:

https://teachersthriving.com/australian-teachers-work-longer-hours-than-doctors/

https://www.bls.gov/opub/mlr/2008/03/art4full.pdf

https://www.oecd-ilibrary.org/docserver/eag_highlights-2014-26-en.pdf?expires=1605742263&id=id&accname=guest&checksum=0A3A731E365AE56E4EE0FE4B52C36351

f) **it is an occupation one can fall back into when sick of current employment**. There is an old saying that 'those who can't do take up teaching'. I have never liked this comment because it often came from very bigoted people who 'could not do' their own job and would probably be even worse teachers. However, some university-trained people decide to quit their previous profession and, after a very short training course, do join the teaching profession. Often, with some enthusiasm and a positive attitude towards teaching, they become good teachers because they also bring some practical experiences from the 'real world' and their previous profession with them. This is especially true of people coming from technical occupations were there has been considerable 'hands-on' experience. Sometimes their enthusiasm is diminished when they face the classroom for the first time or find that teaching is harder than they first thought. A former colleague of mine was just such a case. He had been a physicist in the nuclear laboratory of a large hospital and had become bored with the daily task of checking the large number of staff personal radiation counters. His knowledge of nuclear physics was excellent but he had forgotten some of the finer points of chemistry. In one laboratory session at the school, he had used an excessive amount of an explosive mixture and had caused a significant explosion which set fir to the classroom and terrorised his tough class of boys. Luckily no one was hurt, but he decided that teaching was a dangerous health hazard and so returned to the relative safety of radioactivity. Too bad, he had the potential for being a great chemistry teacher and his experiment was reproduced every year as a memorial to his enthusiasm.

1.4 So what is teaching?

Teaching is a personal and emotional process whereby a person passes on society's knowledge, skills and attitudes to others through effective communication.

It usually involves:

- preparing and planning lessons and curricula;

- using effective communication to give the lesson content with regard to individual differences within the class;

- managing the classroom and the behaviour of the students with care and compassion;

- identifying risks to the students and to self in both the classroom and during external activities;

- being a sound role model, showing good moral character and empathy;

- providing pastoral care as needed;

- liaising with parents as part of the three-way education of the child;

- assessing student outcomes and their general development;

- supporting the school's administration and being part of the school's development; and

- interacting with the wider community when appropriate.

1.5 Being a good teacher

This sometimes is not easy, especially if one is in a 'challenging school' (read 'tough students') with a non-supportive school administration. Then it is a matter of surviving in one's own classroom which is important for the students as well as for yourself.

In a good school, the qualities of a good teacher will be found throughout the school and will probably be driven by a combination of a supportive and wise administration, the general camaraderie and cooperation of one's colleagues and the positive interaction between and with the students.

In brief, a good teacher should:

- know their job;

- know their students;

- know themselves; and

- keep their own problems and bias out of the classroom.

Knowing the job of teaching covers many aspects; the art and skills of teaching, a wide understanding of the subject matter to be taught, and general a good, broad knowledge of the requirements and norms of society.

Knowing the students goes beyond the simple statistics of the name, age and parental details and other such information usually found in the student records. Teaching is a very personal occupation and even the toughest student appreciates this and often needs the personal understanding that a good teacher can give. Teaching can be a clash of personalities or an enhancement and development of personalities depending upon the teacher's attitude and desire to 'get to know' the individuals within their class.

Knowing themselves, teachers are best able to cope with the many difficulties within the school situation as well as knowing their strengths and weaknesses. Bad teachers sometimes are those personalities who are not happy within themselves; they may feel inferior within the social context of the school or feel that they are superior to it and treat the students accordingly.

Keeping their own problems out of the classroom can often be difficult, especially if many of the problems are associated with the school. Teaching can often be considered as a branch of the acting profession as one sometimes has to put one's own difficulties aside and establishing a 'teaching persona'; sometimes exaggerated and a source of motivation in the classroom. In my last school, I was considered to be the resident eccentric scientist in the school and the odd classroom weird experiment, unexpected minor explosion and generally having an element of fun in teaching was a strong motivating influence on the students.

Sometimes, professional bodies, especially those controlling the school within a government system or even in a large, corporate school will provide 'guidelines' for what is expected of their teaching staff. Unfortunately, these can consist of copious pages of jargon listing a detailed range of expectations usually in educational terms which the young teacher has difficulty in reading, let alone trying to meet. Some 'School Rules' are the same and it is a wonder that any student is able to behave perfectly. They are like the many pages of fine print provide as helpful 'guidelines' in insurance policies, hire purchase agreements and solicitor's letters.

To be a good teacher one must:

- like to interact with students in a positive way;

- have empathy for their students and their problems and be a good communicator;

- be kind, courteous and tolerant;

- have a good personal knowledge of the subject matter and of society in general; and above all

- have a good sense of humour and don't take oneself too seriously.

On this last point, it should be pointed out that students both individually and as a group are extremely perceptive and are always looking for some personality or physical defect of the teacher to exploit. A teacher who takes themselves too seriously and sets themselves apart from their class will soon find this student predation, even in good classes, being used to their disadvantage.

Students love the use of 'nicknames' for their teachers and these can be of endearment or can be used in a derogatory manner, sometimes openly to harass the unfortunate. As the resident 'mad scientist' the word 'Doc' would often be used to refer to me, or as I commanded the school's Naval Cadet Unit and would wear my officers' uniform in class on Mondays, I would sometimes be greeted on a full school assembly by a loud 'aaaaargh! Reddog the Pirate'. This usually would be answered by my threat to have the entire student body 'keelhauled' after lunch which would raise a laugh throughout the assembly. Teaching can be a lot of fun if there is a friendly but controlled interaction with the students.

1.6 Discipline and support

Teachers are expected to maintain a good standard of control in their classroom and about the school.

The ideal teacher will be firm without being aggressive nor abusive and show an unbiased fairness to all students regardless of their level of behaviour, gender, race and religion. To do this, some teachers also need to be great actors. In simple terms, the discipline within a school is determined by:

- its client community;

- the administration;

- the behaviour of the students;

- the parents; and

- the teaching staff.

Total school discipline and its organisation culture can vary from a completely dysfunctional school where the administration has disowned any responsibility to control the students who are usually dominated by a small minority of miscreants. Staff are left to their own devices and often suffer psychological, verbal and physical abuse by the students. There is often little assistance from middle level superiors who either lack the ability to offer help or are frightened to 'make waves' and thus limit their chances of promotion.

In such schools, the teacher is very much alone in their classroom and must depend upon their personality to develop some sort of safe, working relationship with their class. Of the seven schools in which I taught, I was lucky enough to only be in two such dreadful schools; one as a young teacher and the other as an experienced Head of Department.

In the first of these, my second school, the Headmaster was totally unsuited for the job and was culturally out of his depth in the local community. An older man, he had few social graces; 'just a boy from the bush' was his own self appraisal, and he had a genius for offending everybody, especially parents. As it was a boys' school, disciple was expected to be maintained by the use of the cane which only harmed the good student who fell afoul of an abusive teacher and had no effect on the student thugs who were causing all of the trouble. I was a young teacher and finding little support, retreated to my classroom and maintained my own version of class humane discipline. For most days this was good enough as I had two advantages: firstly, the school had been 'seeded' from my own school which had been a State-run selective boys' high school and so I knew many of my student's older brothers (and regrettably some of my old teachers, were now 'colleagues'); and secondly, I had been brought up in a tough neighbourhood so that I thought along similar lines to many of my students, many of whom came from Sydney's tough dockside suburbs.

My personal attitude had also come from my previous school which had set the standards for my entire teaching career. The Headmaster here was well ahead of his time and the school was set in a community of Public Servants, many of whom were in the military. I had started teaching at nineteen and so was only a few years older than the teenagers I taught. It was a great school with little if any discipline problems. Fifty years later, I met most of my first students at a reunion of the school which had long since been closed down. The students, however had maintained a close camaraderie after they had left school. An ex-student explained to me why I was a popular teacher. I had caught him smoking with his friends under the floor of my classroom and they had expected to be expelled. I simply thought that the sight of these scared teenagers coughing with smoke was more humorous than a threat to school discipline so I laughed, confiscated their cigarettes and returned them to their places in the class, much to the delight of their classmates who gave them a good-natured hard time. The ex-student, now a Photographer of international reputation, told me that I was liked because <u>I thought like them and knew what problems they were experiencing.</u> That was how I had always thought but it took fifty years for me to be aware of it consciously.

My second tough school came many years later when I changed states for family health reasons and had to restart my career as a Probationary Teacher. I had previously spent the last twenty years teaching, seven of which was as a Head of Department ready to take a job as Deputy Principle. Luckily, after three years of low salary and menial school tasks, I passed the official inspections and was again promoted as Head of Department to yet another 'challenging school'. This was in a tough, working class neighbourhood in the next city a good drive from my home. I had no problem with that as I found that I could communicate with the students here as well. There were two major instances about discipline in this school worth noting as illustrations of what to do and what not to do.

The first came from my new 'extra-curricular' activity which all schools usually have and must be staffed. I had been 'volunteered' to supervise the sports afternoon in roller skating as no one else would do it. This was an activity which the tough, non-sportsmen of Grade 10 had taken on as their gang activity. At the rink, shared with another tough local school, the teachers of the other school and my own colleagues all retreated to the rink's café, and had very much a 'circle the covered wagons' mentality. I in my innocence went onto the rink to skate with my students much to their sadistic glee. The students were not aware that in my tough childhood neighbourhood, I would roller skate at night around the darkened streets and sometimes grab a lift behind passing trucks. Seeing a teacher on the rink meant that I now became a common target for both school's students who did all that they could to trip me up. Not a chance! I easily jumped over the extended legs, spun around and skated backwards grinning at my shocked ambushers. Then a fight broke out on the rink, started by some thug from the other school. As my school had the worst reputation in the district, they were targeted by the manager for eviction. I stepped in (or rather skated in) and explained what had happened. The other school was thrown out. Soon I was surrounded by the thugs from my school, most aged about fifteen but bigger and tougher than I. Their leader put his arm around my shoulders and said:

"You're O.K, George (my nickname). You're one of our gang now. Any strife at school will be handled by us, See?" My discipline at that school suddenly improved and no one dared give me a hard time. <u>I was one of them whilst retaining my teacher's authority</u>.

The second discipline event at that school began when a young female student came to my HOD office with a note from one of my teachers. He had been given my old Grade 10 class by the incompetent old deputy Headmaster who had noted that they were well behaved with me and so would suit this new teacher. The note read:

'The class is revolting. Come now!'

I was rather staggered by this note and the look of frustration on this messenger's face; a young student whom I knew to be an excellent young person. So, I quickly stopped what I was doing and ran after my messenger of gloom. I could hear the class as soon as I entered the long corridor of the Grade 10 Block. Noise of yelling, thumping and above all of this a VERY loud accented voice yelling:

"You vill be quiet! You vill sit down! Shut up!'

It sounded like a scene from Arnold Schwarzenegger's movie *Kindergarten Cop*. Entering the room, I found the students running across desks, throwing paper and generally yelling at the tops of their teenage voices. They HAD revolted.

There was a mad rush to regain their seats as I entered. Afterall, I was the HOD and had been a good teacher with them previously. They had resented this exchange of teachers and their new teacher's concept of Germanic discipline. I quickly quietened the class and gave them some written work to do and gently took Arnold outside the room. He explained in a very loud voice with eyes bulging out of a very red face that he expected them to be silent at all times, give him respect and simply copy their textbook diligently without comment. I suggested that he go to the Staffroom and have a coffee and then I returned to the class. There, the Class Captain, my previous messenger of doom, explained that they were unhappy at being treated badly by such a fanatical disciplinarian who had no personal relationship with the students in the class and generally had an aggressive personality (or words to that effect). I gave them a gentle reminder of their obligations as students and requested that they should give him another chance if I could persuade him to relax a little. They agreed and as the period bell had just sounded, I dismissed them and went in search of Arnold. Over a coffee and a lot of blustering, yelling and bulging of eyes, I suggest that he should relax and treat his class more humanely, giving him the opportunity to sit in on my classes to get some ideas. He was a Probationary Teacher and so he reluctantly agreed, especially after I mentioned quietly that I would visit his class on some future occasions to 'give him some support'. He did not relax, lasted a week and then resigned.

The point of these examples is that it is up to the teacher to develop a 'class persona' which would allow for a good, happy learning environment.

A very wise Principal in one of my later good schools had the philosophy that there should be only two 'School Rules':

1. **a school should be a safe, happy place**; and that

2. **no one has the right to interfere with anyone else's education**.

These rules applied to everyone in the school community, students, staff and parents and were well-known to all. Everyone thought that they made good sense and tried to follow them. The community was a small, go-ahead farming community who valued education and there was no doubt why this school achieved some of the best results in the entire State.

Unfortunately, there will always be some students within the class who have very little self-control and will not settle down when requested. I generally had the expectation that if anyone was talking the rest should listen quietly except when they were working on projects or other class work. This rule also applied to me and so <u>listening with full attention should be one of a teacher's main skills</u>.

Some students have emotional or learning problems and tend to be hyperactive. Some tolerance should be given to their condition but the student must be asked in a firm but friendly way to try to control their outbursts. Sometimes, such enthusiasm can be used by the teacher to make such a student more inclusive by 'volunteering' them for some exciting or physical task. In a good class, these students are usually tolerated and some student support is often evident. If the student continually goes beyond the teacher and class expectations of behaviour and they are genuinely disruptive, then they should be quietly separated from the others. This might mean sitting them at the rear of the room so that they cannot attract the gaze of the others and have little opportunity to talk with them. Of course, classwork for these students should continue and the teacher should involve them in class discussion without any hint of victimisation. If the bad behaviour continues from the rear of the room, then the student may have to be sent out of the room.

This would be the ultimate immediate classroom discipline method. The student could be set just outside the room at a desk in a place where they can be seen by the teacher (and regularly checked) and given the class work to complete by the end of the lesson. If this does not work and the student wanders off, makes more noise or disrupts neighbouring classes, then they will have to be sent 'to a higher authority'. Some schools have a 'Time

Out Room' for such students. This is staffed by some poor unfortunate teacher with good control on a rostered system and the students are expected to work quietly. If such a system does not exist then the student should be sent to the Head of Department or even higher along with an explanation why they have been sent. This must be followed up with the superior and if the student is later re-instated in the class, there should be no further retribution. They have done their time – for the time being. Extreme cases must be referred to the Principal and the parents involved.

Teaching is a three-way process involving the student, their parents and the school.

1.7 So what about Instructors?

Throughout this book, I tend to give some general hints for classroom teaching but most of it, making allowances for an adult student body would also apply to that category of educator loosely defined as 'the Instructor'.

Instructors usually are those persons who have some specific expertise which is to be imparted to an individual (as in having a 'Personal Instructor') or to groups of individuals requiring some upgrading of knowledge, skills or even attitudes as in an introductory program in the corporate culture and ways of behaving within an organisation. Usually, discipline is not a major problem as the students are either adults or highly motivated. Exclusion is also a major option.

Instructors could be adults such as in the military, trade-skills organisations, corporate training situations or even with younger people in such voluntary organisations as scouts, military cadets or in environmental groups. The common ground with these organisations is that an instructor is needed specifically to pass on some expertise and that there may or may not be some long-term emotional pastoral care requirement. Of course, such definition changes depending on the nature of the content, the student and the organisation, for example:

- a physical exercise instructor will concentrate on adult body function and fitness;

- a human resources instructor may provide an introductory period of training to new members of an organisation;

- a drill instructor will train recruits in various physical skills; and

- a driving instructor will give a very personal series of lessons in how to operate a motor vehicle or plant equipment.

University and college lectures often vary greatly in their approach to teaching. They could be impersonal instructors, say in a large lecture hall with hundreds of students, to being a personal one-on-one mentor. They may have some natural teaching ability or even have had teacher training and experience or they may be a dysfunctional personality given classes as part of their academic tenure. The latter is usually treated by their adult students in much the same way as they would be in a class of Year 10 predators.

Regardless of the style of teaching, most of the following chapters of this book should be useful.

Chapter Two

Getting Out the Message –

Communication.

2.1 The basics of communication

Communication can take many forms and be directed or incidental. Basically, communications can be:

- verbal or

- non-verbal

In some lessons, lectures and other 'periods of instruction' both of these could be covered in the old-fashioned 'chalk-and-talk' lessons or in a more modern electronic setting, 'Death by Powerpoint'.

I was once told by a superior being (a university Dean of Science) that my role in teaching 'Teaching Method' to post-graduate students was to simply 'stand up there and tell them how to teach'. His view was that teaching was a simple one-way form of verbal communication. He did concede that occasionally some diagram would have to be written up on the blackboard to illustrate a point. Luckily for the students, my colleague and I ignored this directive as we were both experienced classroom teachers and we were able to beg, borrow (and sometimes steal) audio-visual aids to enhance our informal, interactive lectures on how to teach by our own example.

Verbal communication obviously requires the use of language and this can be done well or be a total disaster. Few teacher-training organisations appear to train their students in how to use language properly and without any application to actively teaching. More on that later.

Non-verbal communication often can be used to impart a great deal of information. 'One picture is worth ten thousand words' is a phrase erroneously attributed to the Chinese philosopher Confucius but was probably by Fred R. Barnard who wrote this phrase in 1921. He wrote this in the advertising trade journal *Printers' Ink,* when promoting the use of images in advertisements that then appeared on the sides of streetcars and it is certainly true in education.

Non-verbal communication can take the form of: signs; lists; cartoons (my favourite); body, hand positions and movements; touch (care!); facial expressions; animations; computer simulations and games; sounds, signals and codes such as using flags and flashing lights. Once I was faced with the task of teaching science to a 'slow-learner' group who had been classified as 'intellectually-impaired' simply because they were young migrant children fresh 'off the boat' who did not have a word of English. Most of my lessons were active skill lessons with lots of simple science experiments, carefully demonstrated beforehand and supplemented by hand signals, facial expressions and cartoons on the blackboard. I also taught some impromptu English and as soon as they had some proficiency in this language, had them promoted to main-stream classes.

In general, any act of communication could be represented by:

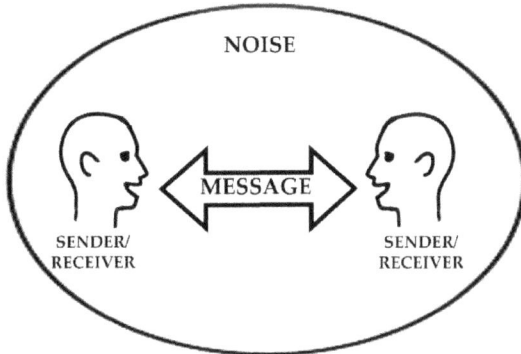

Figure 2.1 Simple elements of communications

In this diagram, communication is simple and two-way with the expectation that each person speaks in turn – often not the case in a classroom!

Poor communication can occur in any of the elements shown in this diagram, such as problems with the sender, the receiver or the message.

2.2 Problems with the Sender

Such problems are often not obvious to the sender but can be a problem for others. It sometimes is a good idea although embarrassing to have a colleague observe one's classes and constructively criticise the delivery. Alternatively, a lesson may be videoed and then analysed. In teacher training, many of these problems are discovered during assessment of practice teaching sessions. Some of the problems in communications due to the Sender include:

a. **use of foreign language** due to the Sender not having the same language as the class. Even if the sender has been trained in this second language, their accent or actual different meaning of terms may not be understood. Even when the Sender has perfect 'class' language, different meanings of terms may cause poor communications e.g. trying to obtain a dressing gown in a Chinese hotel was useless until I asked for a bath robe. If one is conscious of such confusion, then further practice in the local dialect is required. On the other hand, I have relatives who speak only Spanish but we communicate perfectly through facial expression, signs and the use of a phone translator.

b. **delivery manner** can sometimes be daunting to students if the Sender is aggressive and whose behaviour does not encourage two-way conversation. An old Army Drill Sergeant comes to mind here. Whilst one must be firm and in control of a class, one can also be polite, tolerant and understanding.

c. **volume of the delivery** may often be too loud to be pleasant or too soft and inaudible. With practice, the appropriate volume for a particular room and audience soon develops. For a large auditorium or outdoor excursion, a microphone and amplifier is recommended.

d. **speed of the delivery** will be either too fast for the class to understand individual words or too slow and boring to gain attention. Some teachers whose classroom language is not their native tongue often talk too fast for full understanding. If anything, the Sender should <u>slow down</u> their speed of delivery slightly, <u>lower their tone</u> and <u>ensure suitable spaces</u> between key words and sentences.

e. **poor modulation** of delivery also results in boredom and inattention. A monotone delivery usually is not as successful as one in which some variation in tone, emphases on key terms and appropriated excitement when appropriate is used. Teachers should be actors and consider the dramatic use of voice along with appropriate facial expressions and body actions. Sometimes a 'pregnant pause' is useful at some dramatic moment.

f. **poor enunciation**, especially of foreign and technical terms can decrease the interest in communications, especially if the class is young and impressionable e.g. dropping letters off words such as the 'g' in 'going' (or worse… use 'gonna') walking etc, the 'h' in words like 'happen', 'half' etc. In some languages such as 'broad' Australian (or 'strine') whole sentences can be full of bad enunciation. Coupled with slang expressions, such communication could almost be incomprehensive to anyone other than the converted e.g. "emma chizit, thim b'tydas?" for "how much are those potatoes?" or "G'dye mite, hey gaan?" for "Good day, mate. How are you going?"

g. **poor grammar** is the death of any delivered sentence and when coming from a so-called 'educated person' it greatly distracts from the message and their credibility. We see it in the media nightly. For example, these include:

- **sloppy terms** and speech such as 'gonna', for 'going to', 'dunno' for 'don't know' and so on. One hears these on the media every day, especially from Sports Commentators;

- **constant use of 'reinforcers'** and 'thought moments' such as '…like', 'you know', 'ummm', 'what's that?' etc. which can be said several times per sentence in everyday conversation. Listen to any teenager talking;

- **double negatives** which are common in pop songs and the like such as "I cain't get no satisfaction";

- **using the wrong verb tense** e.g. "I drive to the store and bought groceries" with 'drive' being present tense and 'bought' being past tense. Substitute 'drove' for 'drive';

- **subject-verb numerical errors** e.g. "Jack and Jill is going up the hill". Use the plural 'are'. Also the annoying use of 'me' such as "Jill and me went up the hill: or "me and Jill went up the hill"; use "I" ;

- **noun-pronoun agreement errors** pronouns should agree with used nouns e.g. "the girls got to the hotel and checked in her hockey sticks" as there are plural nouns 'girls', the 'her' pronoun should also be plural such as 'their';

- **missing subject or verb** in a sentence which should contain both e.g. **"because I went to work"** is an incomplete sentence. What happened when he went to work?

- **run-on sentences** are the bane of authors. It also occurs with people who have no concept of punctuation and talk rapidly. It could be a 'sentence' which has several independent items in it and could be linked e.g. "I went swimming I almost drowned" which should be "I went swimming and almost drowned" or it could be the reverse of this with a very long sentence using many 'ands' to link many independent thoughts. Teachers who think faster than they can put it into words are sometimes guilty of talking fast and non-stop by linking their many thoughts with multiple 'ands' or 'buts'; and

- **misplaced or dangling modifiers** often confuse the listener by what or who is being done by whom. Something which modifies an action should be close to that action e.g. "sleeping in the orchard, the serpent stung me.' (William Shakespeare). So, who was sleeping in the orchard, the snake or me?

For further details on grammar see the following website ('Oxford Guide to English Grammar' by John Eastwood):

https://www.uop.edu.jo/download/research/members/oxford_guide_to_english_grammar.pdf

h. **use of profanities and idioms** can be offensive and confusing and should be excluded.

Unfortunately, some people who use such terms in their daily speech can find their removal difficult. Remember that there are some terms which may be used in one culture are unacceptable in others. As a mild example, consider the term 'rubber' which can mean 'condom' in American but an 'eraser' in other English. I remember a young American Exchange Student who almost fell off his chair when a good-looking female student asked him if he had a rubber (i.e., an eraser). Other terms may have racial undertones and common texting abbreviations such as OMG etc should be avoided.

i. **direct eye contact** is often given as the appropriate communication bridge when talking to another person. Looking over their head or at the floor or worst still, with one' eyes closed, is often considered a distractor in personal communication. In most cases this is valid, but remember that there are some cultures, especially indigenous cultures, which consider direct eye contact aggressive or disrespectful. Some African, Hispanic, Asian and Middle Eastern cultures have difficulty with direct eye contact. With a multi-cultural class, it is best to take the lead from students who talk to you.

j. **over use of technical terms** is a great way for the 'expert' to demonstrate their superiority and to create confusion in the class. This also applies to non-verbal equations, symbols and diagrams. Remember that teaching is the art of translating what the expert knows into language which the students can understand. If technical terms and symbols are a necessary part of the lesson then these must be explained in simple terms and practiced. Solicitors, politicians, medical practitioners and academics often have this problem, especially in their writing.

2.3 Problems with the Receiver

The Receiver is usually the student but in a good two-way communication process he/she could also be the teacher. Assuming that the teacher is empathetic, tolerant, a good listener and has a good command of the student's language, then some of the problems which a Student/Receiver could have include:

a. **language difficulties** due to their lack of skills in the language used in the classroom or even the common idioms used by the others. Being aware of such difficulties in the students is at least a starting point for a teacher who could spend extra time in explaining concepts individually to the student. In a multicultural class where there are likely to be many such difficulties, the teacher should keep language simple and support verbal communication with non-verbal forms. It would be more appropriate for schools to have special classes for students with local language difficulties;

b. **intellectual difficulties** do not only refer to students with diminished mental ability but generally to the overall intellectual ability and level of understanding of the entire class. This also relates to age as well and it can be a problem for an adult teacher with a good education to reduce their terms and concepts to those which students can understand. Also, within any comprehensive classroom of mixed ability, the teacher should also make provision for assisting the less able as well as providing more challenging tasks for those students of better ability. In some schools. Especially in the past, classes in each year or age group were often graded in terms of ability. This allowed for remediation teaching and the use of special expertise and resources for slower learners and also extra work at a more difficult level for more able students. There were good and bad arguments for such grading, but the current trend seems to be classes of mixed ability to reflect the nature of society and provide better tolerance and social interaction between the students. Talking down to students is also annoying;

c. **personality differences** of the student due to their psychological nature and their up-bringing which can affect their ability to fully understand what is being taught but also in their own self-control within the classroom. There may also be problems associated with their home life which can carry over into the classroom. An authoritarian or abusive parent or both parents will greatly change the student's outlook on education as a whole, especially if they find a similar personality clash with authoritarian teachers and school administrators;

d. **cultural differences** of students often moderate how they receive information. Many students come from families where their culture requires that they pay attention to teachers and do their best to understand. They may constantly ask questions or sometimes not ask any at all so as not to 'lose face'. Other cultures are not so diligent and have cultural backgrounds which see education as relatively unimportant; and

e. **financial situation** of the parents can be an inhibition in communication if the student cannot have access to the appropriate classroom or outdoor resources. Usually such problems can be overcome, but there is a direct correlation between the socio-economic background of the student and their communication, motivation and learning in class.

2.4 Problems with the Message

This is where careful planning and a good knowledge of the nature of the students can turn a poor lesson into a good one. The most common problems with the message which is to be delivered in the classroom are:

a. **the content is not at the appropriate level** of the student. With teachers new to the class, the content may often be pitched at a higher level than the students can understand. Hopefully there will be some guidance from Work Programs developed from a Syllabus to alert the teacher to the age level of the content and there should also be some guidance from the school as to the general ability of the class;

b. **the message is too long** and so its impact is lost. Timing of lessons is important and only comes with experience. Also, it is common for a prepared lesson to be only partially completed. This may occur when the interaction with the class becomes more important and new areas to explore are introduced. These lessons can be highly motivational and of better value to the students than a teacher's insisting on formally completing a prepared lecture as such. The worst calamity is for a new teacher to under-prepare a lesson and suddenly find that there is a large gap at the end with nothing to put into it. Experienced teachers rarely have this problem, but in an emergency, there should be a few revision questions, a word game or some other appropriate student activity at hand.

c. **the delivery is only pitched at one level** and does not allow for the differences in ability and understanding within the class, especially in a mixed-ability group. Whilst the message may be prepared at an appropriate level, provision must be made for more simple explanations for lower ability students and extensions prepared for those of higher ability; and

d. **the method of the delivery is not varied** and is boring because it lacks appropriate examples, illustrations, changes in pitch, appropriate audio-visual aids, and does not involve student participation. A lecture given in a monotone can be the death of any lesson.

2.5 The problem of Noise

Noise can be defined as any distracting element which interferes with the delivery of the message. The most common example of noise in the classroom include:

a. **disruptive students** will greatly interfere with the giving of the lesson. An experienced teacher will put a stop to such behaviour quickly and gently with little time lost. If the disruption comes more frequently and from one or several students, then these students should be separated, say at widely-spaced seating at the back of the room or if severe with total exclusion from the classroom depending upon school policy. Any student sent out must still be supervised and given work, so it is best to keep such students in the room;

b. **environmental factors** can limit the effectiveness of the communication due to unsatisfactory temperature, problems with lighting, smell, real noise, lack of cleanliness, poor building structure and the like. To some extent a teacher may limit or overcome some environmental issues but they may need to be addressed on a whole school basis. I once taught in a school which was centrally heated in winter but this heating could only be turned on after a certain date. We had heavy snow and temperatures below freezing a week before this date and the authorities were inflexible. Imagine a class of shivering students wrapped in fire blankets and warming their hands around the pitiful flames of many small laboratory Bunsen burners! and

c. **other external factors** can sometimes be disruptive such as if the class or teacher next door is causing a rumpus or the laboratory across the corridor has overdone the manufacture of a bad gas. A gentle word may have to be given to such colleagues! Other infrequent disruptions (in most schools) may also include evacuations, fire alarms or an over-use of the school's intercom system by the Principal or his secretary (a common event in one of my schools so we disconnected the loudspeaker).

2.6 Communications networks

Communications within an educational context are never simple because a true educative process involves the interaction of more than two people and with often multiple pathways.

Communication should also be two-way with a dynamic civilized interaction between students and teacher. In the old, 'traditional' past such as in my early childhood, classroom communication was usually only one-way and student interaction was often seen as something to be punished. Later, as a teacher, this same principle seems to also be applied to staff with the Principal giving instructions down the line with little feedback coming from the staff. A very poor situation!

Organisational communication theory recognises several network systems which could also be applied to schools and other educational institutions. These are given in Figure 2.2:

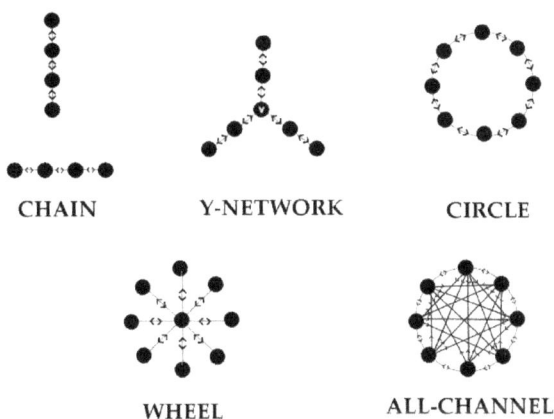

CHAIN   Y-NETWORK   CIRCLE

WHEEL   ALL-CHANNEL

Figure 2.2 Communications networks

These diagrams are also rather simplistic and show two-way communications between all parties. Nor do communication networks always stay fixed, but may change depending upon the circumstance. Each network may also have some internal modification, change in direction of the message flow and the number of parties involved in the network. A simplified description of these networks and their application in Education is given below in Table 2.1:

NETWORK	DESCRIPTION	APPLICATION
Chain	In chain network, communication travels up and down through the hierarchy. Each person communicates with only the person directly above or below in terms of reporting relationships, rigidly following the formal chain of command.	Typical of many school administrative structures where the Principal is remote. The pathway of communications is usually downward with formal methods required to communicate upwardly. 'Gate-keepers' such as over-zealous secretaries can stop messages upward and messages may also get distorted when passed along the chain laterally.
Y-network	In the Y network, the flow of communication resembles an upside-down Y; information flows upward and downward through the hierarchy, widening to encompass the number of staff reporting to a supervisor.	Similar to some models with schools whereby teaching staff communicate to the administration via an intermediary.

Circle	In a circle network, parties communicate only with adjoining members of the organization but not with others in the group.	Rarely has great application within a school but could be used in networks in which specific messages are passed on in a serial way such as official documents.
Wheel	In a wheel network, information flows to and from a single person. Parties in the group communicate primarily with that person rather than with each other. Such a communication network is a fast means of getting information to staff members, since the person at the hub of the wheel can do so directly and efficiently. The wheel network relies on the leader to act as the central conduit (channel) for the entire group's communication.	A reasonable model for lower-tier management such as Subject Heads who need to get information out to their staff. Could also be used in a modified way as a common classroom model centred around the teacher, but each member in the wheel would have two-way communications with each other as well.

All-channel	In an all-channel network, communications flow upward, downward and laterally among all members of the group. This pattern of communication supports egalitarian participation and fosters cooperative efforts.	A good classroom model if the teacher held a central and controlling position. The emphasis being on control of the communication between outlying parties (students) so that two-way communication can occur freely without interruption.

Table 2.1 Communication networks attributes

It is an interesting exercise to analyse the communication networks within a school's organisation and see where you fit in. Even within each class there would be sub-surface communication networks with some students dominating communications over others, especially those who do not communicate freely. A good teacher will soon find out how the class communication system works and spread their own communications to the class in a uniform and fair manner. Some students may also need some special care in getting them to communicate freely such as having them simple questions, asking their opinion and perhaps getting them to become part of group communication activities, but one must be careful in over forcing shy students beyond their acceptable limits.

2.7 Questioning technique.

Using questions and responding to answers is a major skill of any educator and should be a comfortable and common aspect of every classroom. The teacher/instructor should develop a classroom environment in which students should feel comfortable about asking and answering questions.

Some basic concepts which may be useful for a teacher in asking questions is given below in Table 2.2:

CONCEPTS	REASON
1. Ask the question – pause – and <u>then</u> nominate the student.	This forces the entire group to think of the answer.
2. Make questions clear and to the point – no 'multi-barrel' questions.	There should be no doubt in the student's mind as to the question.
2. Spread the questions around the room equally.	Favourites, especially in gender, race and ability are not acceptable.
3. Insist that the answers are given audibly in the common language of the class.	Good training for the person and so that all can hear the answer.

4. Do not test the powers of student expression too far.	Highly involved or technical questions are difficult to answer.
5. Never question on manipulative skills	Skills are best demonstrated.
6. Avoid the 50/50 question.	This encourages student guessing.

Table 2.2 Some concepts in giving questions.

Naturally, the good teacher will ask questions so that the student will not feel intimidated nor that they are being bullied and receiving undue attention. If a student cannot answer a question, then one should move on so that the student does not feel any shame nor retribution from his/her peers.

If a student cannot answer, or gives an incomplete answer then it should not be an opportunity for ridicule. Rather than calling young Bloggs a moron, the teacher can ask another student their opinion of the answer or to give their own answer in a friendly manner. Ridicule of anyone is not acceptable in the classroom. If several of the students cannot answer the same question, then it indicates that perhaps the teacher did not make the point in the first place. Some humility here is required with the main point being revised. Poor

Bloggs can then be given another chance with a simple question 'to save face'.

Students should also be encouraged to ask questions in class – in fact this is one of the main teaching strategies that a good teacher should develop. After class questions from shy or curious students should also be fostered. Some basic concepts about how a teacher/instructor should answer questions are given below in Table 2.3:

CONCEPTS	REASON
1.Encourage question	Students must feel that they can freely ask questions if in doubt
2.Repeat the question	Emphasises its importance and ensures that the others have also heard it
3.Give the question on to the class – if no correct answer, give it.	Provides good group interaction and helps to find what students know.
4.Answer all sincere questions,	Keep the answer short. If personal, say so.
5.Never bluff.	If you don't know, say so. Students do not respect bluffing.
6. Avoid the 'Red Herring' question which has nothing to do with the lesson	Gently put it aside until after the lesson. You can also ask the student to look it up.

Table 2.3 Some concepts in answering questions.

Chapter Three

So, what's the Point? - Objectives for Learning

GRADES

3.1 Need for a clear direction

Students need to have a full and very clear understanding of what they are to learn. There can be no doubt as to the general purpose of any lesson, the details of what is being taught and why.

Any lesson should have a well-defined AIM. This is a general statement of intent which describes what the learner will achieve or what the teacher/instructor will deliver by the end of the lesson.

To achieve this general purpose, the student will have to meet very definite OBJECTIVES. These should be SMART:

S = Specific;
M = Measurable;
A= Attainable;
R =Realistic; and
T= Time-Appropriate.

Specific details must be included in the objectives stated at the beginning of the lesson. They should be so stated as to be able to be directly measured by some form of assessment item at a later date and they should be attainable by the age and level of ability of the student. With this in mind, the objectives of the lesson should be realistically achieved and within the given time stated.

To meet these criteria therefore, objectives should also be kept simple and few in number, perhaps no more than say, four or five per lesson.

For example:

the **Aim** of this chapter is to outline and explain the need for clear direction in lessons.

Objectives: - by the end of this chapter, the reader should be able to:

1. Distinguish between an aim and an objective;

2. Construct simple objectives using key verbs;

3. Apply this knowledge to write objectives for any type of lesson;

4. List some appropriate key verbs for different types of objective or performance criteria; and

5. Discuss methods of assessment suitable for some stated objectives.

Notice the key elements in these stating objectives: a simple and clear action to be taken for each and a very well-defined time limit for their achievement. Having too many objectives, especially if vague and with multiple meanings tends to confuse students and are generally unachievable in the time given for the lesson. A few simple objectives given for the lesson can not only be achieved but also probably assessed by informal questioning at the end of the lesson or during it at different stages as each objective has been achieved.

These principles can also be used in the writing of larger work units for entire topics in which both the number of simple objectives and the time for their completion has been increased.

3.2 Thinking about objectives

Always keep in mind that classroom objectives should be kept simple and have no doubt as to their intent both for the teacher and for the students. They will state clearly ONE goal and the time by which it will be achieved. The SMART concept should be applied when designing or constructing appropriate objectives.

Vague 'motherhood' statements designed to impress other educators (especially supervisors) or which are used through a poor understanding of their true intention do not help anyone. The other principle to keep in mind is the KISS principle (Keep It Simple, Stupid!).

As a general rule of thumb when constructing objectives is to ask the question 'how will it be assessed?' For example, the vague objective which starts with the key term 'to appreciate…blah blah etc' begs the question of how one is going to test this appreciation after the lesson? Theoreticians may respond:

'Oh well, that's simple. Give them an Opinion Survey."

Well, why not write THIS as the objective e.g. 'by the end of the lesson, students will be able to complete an opinion survey on blah, blah etc.' The responses to such a survey will certainly show how the students have generally appreciated the topic.

Similarly, the vague objective that 'students should know about blah, blah etc' also doesn't help the assessment of such an objective. How do you know that they know? Testing this 'knowledge' objective would need some test items anyway which could have been originally stated as more appropriate objectives in the first place, such as 'list', 'define', 'explain',' describe', 'define' and other more direct key verbs.

Think about it! How do you develop a practical set of objectives for a lesson or even a larger sequence of lessons? I have had to construct workable educational objectives at the class level for my own classes, at the school teaching program level for my staff and in designing the State curriculum as Head of its Curriculum Committee in my subject area. It sometimes is not easy!

3.3 Types of Objectives

In thinking about the objectives for a particular lesson, one needs to consider the need for type and variety of what the students must learn and do in the classroom.

There have been several attempts to define and classify educational objectives at the educational research level, with the most notable being that of Benjamin Bloom (1913 – 1999), an American educational psychologist. His classification system or 'taxonomy' came out in 1956 which was later revised in 2001. It has been widely used by many educators and there also has been considerable criticism about its application in K-12 classrooms. A discussion on Bloom's taxonomy (classification) is beyond the scope of this book, but some additional reading for those who are curious can be found at the following sites:

http://www.nwlink.com/~donclark/hrd/bloom.html

https://www.virtuallibrary.info/blooms-taxonomy.html

https://www.d41.org/cms/lib/IL01904672/Centricity/Domain/422/BloomsTaxonomy.pdf

It is import not to be bogged down by too much educational research, but rather consider what it suggests and make use of the findings in a practical way. Bloom's committee proposed that educational objectives could be categorised into three Domains:

1. Cognitive: which considers **Knowledge (K)** of what is to be taught;

2. Psychomotor: or the **Skills (S)** to be taught; and

3. Affective or the **Attitudes (A)** or emotions which should come from the teaching.

Using this system, one now has to look at a future lesson and try to develop appropriate objectives which would suit the topic, the age and ability level of the class. This may be supported by curriculum documents such as a syllabus or subject teaching program which also may use the KSA approach.

One practical way of doing this is to consider the specific lesson topic, review any curriculum documents and then:

1. think specifically about the specific CONTENT of what the students are to learn. This will help to define the Knowledge Objectives;

2. think about any practical work, writing tasks, mathematical processes needed etc. and any other activities which the students will have to perform in gaining this knowledge. These will define the Skill Objectives; and

3. think about what emotional benefits or change in mental attitude which could come about by learning this content performing these skills. Hopefully, this will involve an attitude change.

Remembering the SMART guidelines, one can then construct an appropriate overall general Aim and then Lesson Objectives for knowledge, skills and attitudes using the time factor (e.g. 'by the end of the lesson, students should...') and practical key verbs for each objective.

I am not convinced about the importance of a hierarchy of objectives, often quoted in the knowledge domain of Bloom's Taxonomy, but rather see that learning takes place independently of such hierarchy and often in a random way depending upon the motivation and interaction between the teacher and the student.

However, when looking for the appropriate 'key verb' with which to construct a useful objective, one must consider the age and ability level of the student who must understand the meaning of such verbs. For example, it would be meaningless to construct an objective using the term 'analyse' for very young students who may not have the full comprehension of the meaning of the term. In the case of younger students or those with limited ability, the objectives should be given in very simple form. For older students and those of excellent ability then it would be very appropriate and indeed desirable to use some of the so-called 'higher order' thought process verbs.

Still, Bloom's Taxonomy is useful when trying to construct a range of objects so that any unit or lesson objectives are not littered with vague terms such as 'to know' or to 'understand' and so on.

3.4 Constructing objectives in each of the domains.

3.4.1 The Knowledge (Cognitive) Domain

There seems to have been a great emphasis in thinking about what knowledge is to be imparted to the student. In the early days of my career, one did not have to think about objectives nor domains. The syllabus for each subject was given as a sequential list of desired knowledge only.

Moreover, there often was an accompanying document called 'Notes on the Syllabus' which expanded this content greatly, so that the lazy teacher needed only to copy these notes onto the chalkboard and perhaps request some additional reading and exercises from the textbook. Skills came incidentally from any recommended 'practical work' or the activities given in the syllabus. If the students derived any long-term emotional response or set of attitudes from such teaching, then that would be a bonus.

Bloom, and later modifiers to his taxonomy, have identified several types of knowledge objectives. These and some examples of useful verbs to use are given in the following Table 3.1:

	SUB-DOMAIN	MEANING	SOME KEY VERBS/TERMS
I N C R E A S I N G C O M P L E X I T Y	**Basic Knowledge**	Basic facts, terms, definitions, names, lists etc which are simply to be remembered in the future.	list, name, define, sequence, recite, label, find, state, recall, give the meaning of.
	Comprehension	Requires some true understanding of knowledge or abstract concepts and may involve some student-evolved descriptions, translations and interpretation of the main ideas.	explain, rewrite, interpret, outline, discuss, relate, distinguish, restate, translate, compare, contrast, describe.
	Application	Uses new knowledge to solve problems, using rules and techniques involving new situations.	solve, show, use, illustrate, calculate, complete, examine, classify, predict.
	Analysis	Examination of information which can then be broken down into important concepts, motives or causes.	conclude, categorise, identify, advertise, separate, differentiate, separate, infer.
	Synthesis	Combining facts to construct new information, plans, abstract concepts and solutions.	evolve, build, design, compose, create, summarize.
	Evaluation	Judge and defend or reject the validity of information based on given factual evidence.	select, choose, criticise, justify, verify, give arguments for/against, rate, defend, draw conclusions,

Table 3.1 Knowledge Objectives and some key words and terms

In most cases there may not be a need to sub-divide the knowledge objectives and so the key verbs or terms can be used in the construction of more general objectives. It is often a source of frustration and academic debate when people attempt to define or use key words out of context when it is not required. Also, it is quite possible to use the same key verb or term in constructing an objective from different sub-domains e.g. one can test the comprehension of a student by getting them to simply rewrite some description from memory, requiring only their basic **comprehension** of the subject matter e.g. '**Rewrite** a short account of how Columbus found the New World.'

Or they may be given a complex set of ideas such as the main facts about a product and then given the task to **synthesise** these ideas e.g. '**Rewrite** the following data as an article for a motor magazine – streamlined body, 4WD, 200 HP engine, disc brakes, GPS unit, radio/USB player, turbo-charged, vinyl seats for six.'

Some excellent additional information can be found at:

https://www.utica.edu/academic/Assessment/new/Blooms%20Taxonomy%20-%20Best.pdf

3.4.2 The Skill (Psychomotor) Domain

These are objectives designed to focus attention on the learning of physical and other skills. Development of these skills always requires extensive practice and can be measured in terms of precision, speed, or other measurable techniques in the execution of the particular skill. These skills could include:

- the use of specific items of equipment e.g. electronic equipment, scientific equipment, tools and machinery;

- movements or techniques in various sports e.g. gymnastics;

- producing works of art or craft e.g. painting, drawing, wood-turning, pottery;

- dancing, acting and other performing arts;

- construction skills of various types; and other physical skills.

They could also be skills involved in mental processes such as:

- performing mathematical operations;

- creative writing;

- preparation for and planning of new tasks;

- researching libraries and other data bases;

- identifying and classifying specimens and objects;

- working scientifically using deduction and sequence;

- collating data as tables;

- drawing and interpreting graphs; and

- navigation using maps and location plotting; and many more skills involving mental processes and systematic action.

In the school situation, in commerce and industry, the most frequent assessment of skills is through observation and personal critique of the student or group of students performing the set tasks. Constructing objectives which require the student to list the steps in using a skill is invalid as a skill objective and is more suited to that of knowledge.

Whilst there have been attempts to determine sub-domains for skills (Bloom did not attempt this), it generally gets down to the simple task of deciding what manipulative skills the student should have in studying a particular topic. It may mean the use of equipment such as in a laboratory, dance and art studio, gymnasium, test-driving track or industrial workshop and plant operation facility. Key verbs will be determined by the:

- type of equipment used e.g. laboratory equipment, sports equipment, heavy machinery type etc.;

- type of procedure used with it e.g. laboratory or field experiment and/or measurement, use of plant in construction, a dance or stage performance, painting/sculpture in an art studio etc.; and

- purpose of the overall activity or teaching method e.g. as part of normal study, as a one-off accreditation, performance or exhibit.

Some key verbs or terms which may be associated with skills objectives and their assessment (remember SMART) may include:

VERB/TERM	POSSIBLE SITUATION
Use	an item of equipment e.g. a Bunsen burner
Measure	using instruments e.g. a pressure gauge
Perform	a particular operation or part thereof e.g. a double somersault dive
Construct	using a building device or material e.g. line of brickwork.
Operate	devices of various complexity e.g. graphics calculator.
Observe	using equipment to monitor some environment or activity e.g. growth of bamboo plants
Make or Manufacture	some product or item e.g. a short skirt to fit.
Test	using equipment or procedures to prove various factors e.g. blood tests of medical patients.
Separate	using a process or equipment to purify or extract material e.g. freshwater from seawater
Follow Steps	involving some complex process involving sequences.
Assemble (or dismantle)	Involving some physical construction of an item or of its disassembly.
Imitates	The student must follow a complex procedure or motion e.g. gymnastics
Use initiative	Using material or tools to solve a new situation e.g. crossing a ravine using ropes

Table 3.2 Some skill objectives and some key words and terms

There are many different key verbs one can use when constructing specific skill objectives and these depend very specifically on the type of action which is required.

There may be a time limit on the activity such as in practical examination with a school, or it may mean the simple completion of the task to a set of established criteria without any time limit and chances to redo any mistakes.

Performance criteria within the world of Commerce or Industry probably comes into such assessment, but the candidate must be aware of the standards which have been set for the assessment of the performance. Moreover, this assessment may occur instantly following the satisfactory demonstration (or not) of the task or the completion of a work or performance. It may also be an assessment over an extended period of time involving observations and reports by superiors at different stages or the completion of some item, product or process such as a sales record over the month.

Some institutions may also be more specific in their use of objectives and delineate some objectives such as mathematical skills and creative writing.

As with any other skill, these would have to be analysed by the teacher/instructor and the skill components identified e.g. the use of formatting, dramatic construction and the like to write a short story or to use various mathematical concepts to solve a complex relationship.

In teaching skills, especially to younger students, it might be advisable to further break up a skill into any component parts e.g. many sporting techniques require a very specific breakdown such as in golf and how to address the ball, holding the club (and which one to use), the raising of the arm, the downward swing and then the follow through.

The military have a particularly good education system which is used in training troops who may not be highly motivated to do drill on a hot afternoon, or to be able to strip a rifle in the middle of a dark and stormy jungle night. They usually break down the skill during training periods and assign numbers to each part and if there is a particular timing involved overall, this too is broken down. Before the training starts, the instructor will carefully demonstrate the whole procedure and also the separate stages for each number.

For example, consider a new recruit being taught the simple task of saluting…a matter of survival with officious officers lurking about! The whole process is broken down by numbers and the time interval between each section is about one second, given the count of 2-3 ("ta'three"). So, the full sequence of a salute would be:

"On 1, swing the right arm out at right angles to the body in a wide arc with the palm of the hand facing outwards and fingers and thumb together 2-3;

On 2, close the hand and drop it quickly down to the side of the body so that the thumb touches the seam of the trousers."

Quite complex manoeuvres involving many numbers (and 2-3) are usually taught this way with the appropriate **Fault-checking** for individuals who get that part wrong. When that happens, the training stops whilst the individual is given another brief demonstration of the botched manoeuvre and a chance to repeat it. Drill Sergeants can be so kind and helpful!

The military model can be adapted (perhaps without numbers) to most physical skills which are complex and have several natural steps such as in many sports, dance and outdoor activities.

For all skills training at any level, a good, accurate DEMONSTRATION and then much PRACTICE is essential.

3.4.3 The Attitude (Affective) Domain

Teachers and indeed adult instructors also teach incidentally in the hope that their students will also get a good appreciation of their training and any appropriate positive, social attitude which comes from it. In schools, teachers teach this 'hidden curriculum' all of the time in the hope that society's standards in language, behaviour, relationships and respect are passed on as well as the academic subject or specific lessons that they are teaching.

This domain describes how the student or even a group of students develop attitudes or values which are deemed to be socially acceptable. In some schools or institutions there may also be a sub-culture which has other, more socially-negative values which need to be overcome as well, The Affective Domain is concerned with emotions and relationships and so objectives are often difficult to formulate and even more difficult to assess. They are however, worth the perseverance and should be considered before each lesson.

Usually, attitudes and values develop through slow and methodical experience with the real world and by example. This may go through a long process: a student may begin with a passive reception of a desired value such as good behaviour in class; they respond to this as part of the normal learning process; begin to see the usefulness or need for such an attitude; be able to compare their understanding with other circumstances where this attitude is absent or well-developed; and finally accepts the attitude as part of their own characteristic behaviour.

Some school or institutions may formulate the rather vague Attitude objective as 'to appreciate the value of...etc'. This is a very vague statement and again, the question is asked as to how will the teacher be aware that this attitude has been appreciated. People are cunning and given a desired attitude or standard of behaviour to meet, will show this attitude when required. For example, showing students a scene of absolute environmental damage, naturally they will agree with the teacher about how bad the scene is whether they believe in it or not.

Finding absolute key verbs or terms for writing objectives about values and attitudes is difficult. Some terms which could be used include:

- show interest in ….

- develop positive attitudes towards….

- show empathy towards….

- cooperates with ….

- shares the opinion that/of….

- develop values in ….

- believe in….

- is motivated to….

- accepts….

- show independence in ….

- curiosity about ….

Many advocates of writing attitude objectives often use key verbs taken from the knowledge or skill domain but apply them to specific emotions, beliefs of values e.g.

- **reflect** on and describe their personal attitudes and values towards….

- **investigate** and **describe** social and cultural factors….

- **identify** how a range of perspectives can contribute to….

- **develop** and practice strategies for managing competitive situations….

- **recognise** discrimination and support the rights of others in….

….and so on.

Some other examples can be found on the following web sites:

https://www.pediatrics.emory.edu/documents/teaching/resource/Writing%20Learning%20Objectivescurriculum101_8.pdf

https://www.convergencetraining.com/blog/teaching-attitudes-the-affective-domain-of-learning-and-learning-objectives

https://medicine.tufts.edu/sites/default/files/faculty_teaching-writing-objectives.pdf

Assessing attitudes and values is difficult not only in devising test instruments which are valid, but also in the assumption that the student has not developed a mind set in which they 'try to please' or show what they think should be the 'politically correct' response to such items in the test instrument.

Many syllabi institutions opt out of the problem altogether of listing these affective objectives and rely on the teachers' personal interaction with the students to achieve the necessary sought-after social values, interests and positive attitudes. They can do this by:

- being a good role model, acting as an example;

- providing opportunities to discuss social issues and values;

- involving students in suitable and appropriate role playing

- giving unbiased information about controversial issues appropriate to the age, gender and culture of the students; and

- providing opportunities which develop personal interest and hobbies.

One must be careful in treading into the waters of changing attitudes to ensure that the values and attitudes sought after are truly those of valued in the local society and not the biased attitude of the individual teacher or that expressed in a biased media. There also needs to be considerable control as to how values and attitudes are openly expressed in the classroom lest some student wishes to express a negative opinion about age, gender, race or another individual.

Some of the ways in which attitudes and values can be assessed include:

- **direct observation** and notation by the teacher in class and during activities;

- **use of rating scales**, often of the Likert 5-point variety rating scale with 1. Being the worst example of an opinion and 5 being the best;

- **open-ended questions requiring an essay approach.** These can be may reflect what the student thinks that <u>you</u> may want to hear;

- **art work about some controversial issue.** This may be difficult to assess objectively but may show some psychological processes of the student;

- **request for a rank-order** of a given list of values or priorities; and

- **observe a structured debate** on some controversial issue or attitude. This requires some expertise in scoring debates.

Some excellent additional information on using key verbs in writing KSA objectives can be found at:

https://www.utica.edu/academic/Assessment/new/Blooms%20Taxonomy%20-%20Best.pdf

and for a look into the future:
http://www.oecd.org/education/2030-project/teaching-and-learning/learning/attitudes-and-values/Attitudes_and_Values_for_2030_concept_note.pdf

3.5 An example

Consider the task of an instructor who has to prepare a night lecture for young apprentices in the electrical trades about safety. The previous lesson had been about types of electrical components. In this lecture, there will be some demonstrations of equipment and some simple practical activities. It is expected that there will be considerable interaction between the lecturer and the students.

The **Aim** for this lesson may be:

To learn the main rules of electrical safety.

The **Objectives** may be:

By the end of the lesson, students should be able to:

Knowledge:

- **recall** the main rules of safety; and

- **relate** the appropriate rule to situations commonly encountered;

Skills:

- **observe** the main features of operation of some safety appliances; and

- **construct simple circuits** to test aspects of safety.

Attitudes:

- **develop a positive belief** in the need for safety in the workplace; and

- **show initiative** in applying safety procedures in new situations.

There would be other incidental benefits from doing this lesson and generally discussing the students' current work practises.

3.6 Objectives for everybody

When thinking about objectives for a class lesson or unit of work, teachers will do so with the content, skills and attitudes required. An experienced teacher will also have in the back of their professional mind, the capabilities and differences of their students.

There is considerable literature on the individual differences of students, especially those of early school. The developmental psychologist Howard Gardner (1943 -) suggested that people had different approaches or 'intelligences' when it came to learning. His theory of '**Multiple Intelligences**' suggests that these different approaches should be considered when teaching, as students with different ways of thinking and would learn more effectively if these approaches were exploited by the teacher.

Gardner believed that people have different ways of processing information, and these ways are relatively independent of one another. His theory was critical of the standard intelligence theory, which emphasized traditional measures like IQ tests that typically do not take into account any linguistic, and spatial disabilities as well as any cultural differences. A modification of his original work in 1999 would include the 'intelligences' of:

- **Visual-Spatial Intelligence** – those who are good at visualizing things and see concepts and ideas as in terms of images. They understand ideas, even abstract if given visual cues as part of the teaching process. Photos, videos, maps, diagrams and even funny cartoons expressing more difficult relationships are good teaching strategies for these students;

- **Linguistic-Verbal Intelligence** - are students able to use words well, both when writing and speaking and are very good at writing stories, memorizing information, and reading. Word games, mnemonics and stories are good teaching strategies for these students;

- **Logical-Mathematical Intelligence** – these students are good at reasoning, recognizing patterns, and logically analysing problems. They tend to think conceptually about numbers, relationships, and patterns and so work well when given conceptual puzzles, mathematical exercises, scientific experiments and logical problem-solving activities;

- **Bodily-Kinaesthetic Intelligence** – these students are good at activities involving body movement, performing actions, and physical control. They tend to have excellent hand-eye coordination and dexterity and excel at performances, sport and lessons involving manipulative skills. Such students also learn more effectively if they are given a chance to physically handle or operate items within normal classes rather than be told about it or have to read it in a book. They may also be deemed 'hyperactive' by some authorities but given a chance to use their skills in class goes a long way to help their learning;

- **Musical Intelligence** – these students are good at thinking in patterns, rhythms, and sounds. They have a strong appreciation for music and are often good at musical composition and performance. This can be extended to any in-class activity requiring timing, rhythm or use of sounds in general;

- **Interpersonal Intelligence** – such people are good at understanding and interacting with other people and are skilled at assessing the emotions, motivations, desires, and intentions of those around them. They can be called upon in class to resolve conflicts (they make good school leaders) and provide good, balanced opinions during class discussions; and

- **Intrapersonal Intelligence** – these students are uncommonly good at being aware of their own emotional states, feelings, and motivations. They may often be accused of daydreaming or inattention but are good at self-reflection and analysis are useful in class in obtaining an honest opinion or an analysis of their activities such as a debate or scientific experiment.

A chart showing some example of useful objectives classified using some of Bloom's taxonomy and these multiple 'intelligences' of Gardner is given over the next two pages. These are based on theories from educational psychology and should be used as guidelines for good teaching practice.

Bloom Taxonomy →	Gardner's Multiple Intelligences						
	Visual-Spatial Intelligence	Linguistic-Verbal Intelligence	Logical-Mathematical Intelligence	Bodily-Kinaesthetic Intelligence	Musical Intelligence	Interpersonal Intelligence	Intrapersonal Intelligence
Remember e.g. recall, define, name	• Recall meaning of symbols (maps etc) • Identify photos, images of	• Give the meaning of words • Recall words to • Make a summary	• How many.... • Look for patterns.... • Write the formula for... • Recall the expression for....	• Copy movement of • Play charades for • Remember sequence of dance	• Sing (a song) from memory • Identify an instrument playing • Identify the note	• In a group, show how... • Play a game based on recall • In pairs, tell the partner to	• List your strengths & weaknesses, • What are your goals? • What do you think about?
Understand e.g. explain, relate, classify	• Classify using colours etc • Relate images to sounds • Explain a visual memory	• Explain the meaning of terms • Classify as verbs, nouns etc • Paraphrase the text	• Explain the formulae. • Describe the steps for... • Use a table to summarise • Give a conclusion from the data	• Use body movements to • Communicate using sign language • Relate movement to meaning in	• Explain the purpose of (music, song etc)... • Relate the meaning of (music, notes)	• Write simple problems for others to do in.... • Use a group performance to explain...	• Why do you believe in? • How do your experiences relate to...?
Apply e.g. demonstrate, solve, interpret	• Illustrate some written text • Sequence symbols or images • Interpret non-verbal language	• Interpret foreign text • Use mime to show words • Solve riddles	• Draw a flow chart • Construct a time line.... • Calculate.... • Complete the sequence (or matrix)	• Use mime to explain • Demonstrate a dance sequence • Suggest next steps in movement sequence	• Rewrite new words for music • Interpret the use of instruments	• Give a class interview in the role of... • Conduct a group survey on.... • Identify a community social issue and discuss it in the group.	• Use a list of personalities to identify yours Draw a timeline for... • What questions would you ask if...

Table 3.3A: Objectives grid using Bloom's and Gardner's terms

Bloom Taxonomy	Gardner's Multiple Intelligences						
	Visual-Spatial Intelligence	Linguistic-Verbal Intelligence	Logical-Mathematical Intelligence	Bodily-Kinaesthetic Intelligence	Musical Intelligence	Interpersonal Intelligence	Intrapersonal Intelligence
Analyse e.g. Organise, differentiate, test,	• Decode symbols • Organise symbols or letters • Pick the odd image from	• Analyse the purpose of a story, poem • Differentiate the characters in a play, story • Compare or contrast	• Analyse the operations for • Separate fact from fiction in data • Compare and contrast data • Test a formula	• Classify movements • Compare one movement type to another • Break down a movement	• Analyse the notes in • Investigate the style of • Research changes in music • Compare/contrast styles	• Analyse the reasons for • Investigate the needs of others in • How might (an organisation) respond to	• Investigate all of the factors influencing you in.... • Analyse how you think about • Use a diary
Evaluate e.g. defend, support, appraise	• Use criteria to evaluate sketches or photos • Rate or judge images	• Rate the impact of • Pros and cons of a debate • Write references	• Rate the different uses of types of graphs • Appraise methods used in calculations	• Judge a performance or other movements • Rate skills Used in movement	• Rate performances • Critical review of music • Justify criticism of styles of music	• Make a choice between • Offer positive improvements for • Select the best part of (process/life)	• Evaluate the success of your goals in • rank your personal traits
Create e.g. design, construct, assemble	• Take photographs • Make sketches • Construct new signs	• Write a dialogue • Create poems to	• Use theorems or statistics to • Construct tables of data	• Build a small object •	• Write simple sheet music • Play a new piece • Design new songs	• Design a game to simulate • Write a set of rules or criteria	• Design a personal action plan for....

Table 3.3B: Objectives grid using Bloom's and Gardner's terms (continued)

98

Chapter Four

Planning and Preparation.

4.1 The Basics

This is the most important chapter in this book, so read it carefully.

There are three main principles of teaching and instruction:

1. **plan and prepare**;

2. **promote and maintain the desire** to learn; and

3. **confirm** that the main points of the lesson have been assimilated.

All of these principles become part of thorough preparation and planning for a lesson. The first principle is most important and it is highly recommended that new teachers, or those new to the subject matter thoroughly prepare, well in advance. The second principle should be a continuation of a teacher's method and style over time and build up over the term of the teaching. The third principle will occur whenever the teacher wishes to find out if their teaching has been successful. This could be from a few simple questions at the end of the class, the occasional short quiz or test at the end of a topic or more formal examinations, essays, student works and other student output at the end of term.

Preparing and planning is the first consideration. This may include:

- **allocating sufficient time** for the preparation of the lesson. Easy to say for teachers who may have the responsibility and duty of care for a large group of students for most of the day. In Infants/Primary teaching, there are few 'spare periods' in which to prepare lessons so these are usually done after school and at home. In Secondary there may be one or two 'spares', but like all types of K-12 teaching there are other distractions such as basic administration, marking of exams, talking to superiors and parents and a whole host of other items. It gets worse when one is teaching a technical subject and has to assist the Technical Assistant (if any) with maintaining the equipment, ordering, storing and cataloguing stores and ensuring that all workplace health and safety regulations are met. There are also the many needs of pastoral care of students to be given when it is required.

In the real world of commerce and industry, and certainly in the military, allocation of time is a lot more generous with an allocation of often three hours preparation time for every one hour of instruction being common place;

- **determine the logical sequence** of the lesson so that there is a continual flow of learning. The sequence should also be flexible and not necessarily in the same order as that of a text book but suit the class and the natural order of the unit being taught;

- **define aims and objectives** after consideration of the content knowledge, activities to be performed and an understanding of what social issues are involved;

- **revising or learning** the content and requirements of the lesson which may include a thorough reading of the education program or syllabus or reading up from texts or the Internet (if you have it!). Some teachers are crazy and also study at Inservice Courses or do higher university degrees at night; and

- **preparation of teaching aids** including becoming familiar with their operation and their appropriateness for the lesson. More will be said about this later, but it becomes a disaster when a teacher brings in a complex aid and does not know how to operate it or it is used in such a complex way that the main point of the lesson is lost in a technical shamble. With the use of electronic devices such as laptops, mobile (cell) phones, Smart Boards, touch-screen monitors and the like, teachers have to be electronically savvy if they wish to use such teaching aids.

4.2 The Lesson Structure

Every lesson should have a distinct:

1. **beginning**;

2. **middle**; and an

3. **end**

Lessons should not, as some non-teachers think, consist of one long ramble from the time the teacher enters the classroom until the school bell or time tells the students to get up and leave.

Each of the three parts of the lesson are very important:

1. **The beginning** involves consideration of the classroom environment and establishment of what is to be taught.

   It may begin with setting up the room for comfort of the students and ease of teaching. This might mean rearrangement of the seating for a special lesson, such as a small play or group activity or the acquisition of any specialised equipment or testing of a teaching aid.

   With the usual teaching/instruction session, this would also include the entry and seating of the class, establishing order and a greeting and perhaps marking of a roll.

   Experienced teachers may have a seating plan showing where each student sits. This is useful in quickly checking who is missing when the roll is marked. In technical subjects, this also allows for best allocation of equipment and safety in their use. Usually, such allocation should be made initially with a freedom of choice so that students can sit in 'friendship groups' with the proviso that disruptive students could be later relocated. In an open-plan lesson where students are able to sit around where they wish, or outdoors this may not be possible.

It is now that one of the most important steps of the lesson should be taken; the **motivation step** which few teachers seem to use. This assumes that the class is not fully attentive nor ready for the lesson: they may have had another lesson on a different topic and a new start is required; they may have come from another classroom or somewhere else; it may be after a lunch period, after a hard day's work or late at night. Whatever the circumstance, the class needs to be jolted into a high degree of interest in what you are about to teach.

Motivation steps can vary from simple to elaborate. They might include:

- simple showing of some interesting artifact, specimen or curiosity;

- simple slight-of-hand magic trick;

- An appropriate joke or short story;

- A challenge to the class or 'volunteer' to do some small task e.g. tie a certain knot etc;

- A short demonstration;

- display of a photograph or short video clip;

- a quick sketch/cartoon on the chalkboard;

- a throw-on cut-out image on a magnetic whiteboard; or

- some other short, exciting and interesting activity.

A teacher-drawn image drawn instantly on the board, especially a cartoon, always motivates the students because it is coming from a person whom they assume would be incapable of drawing such an image. This is a 'trick of the trade'.

If one is not a good cartoonist then there are ways and means of overcoming this deficiency. For example, one technique which is great for a tired class after lunch or late at night is to:

1. find a popular cartoon, hopefully with some tenuous connection to the lesson topic e.g. the following sketch for an Introduction to Electrical Safety':

This can be drawn freehand as the class is entering the room if you are good enough or:

2. prepared in advance by making a transparency of the sketch (drawn or copied from a book etc.) and projecting it onto the board with an Overhead Projector, or using a slide projector or computer data projector. An old technique before the advent of electronic devices was to cut out the sketch if small (or

make a thin paper reduced copy if large), soak it in cooking oil to make it transparent and then put it into a cardboard slide mount and use a slide projector.

3. then the image is projected onto the board. If it is a chalkboard, use a dark pencil (say, 2B) to make a <u>faint</u> outline of the sketch on the board. If it is a whiteboard, then use a light-coloured crayon. As the class is entering, one simply traces around the outline with a heavy chalk (or whiteboard marker). From the students' point of view, you are drawing a wonderful sketch freehand (oh yeah!)

Of course, if the whiteboard is magnetic (most are) then copy a large version of the sketch onto 'butchers' paper' or a large white sheet and colour it with felt pens, cut around the edges and use tape to stick magnetic strips (i.e. 'fridge magnets' or cut up magnetic sheets used in 'fridge calendars' etc.). Casually throw this cut-out onto the board from a short distance as the class is sitting down. Wow!

A future chapter in this book will help you do your own sketching. I have always found that a freehand sketch on the board really grabs the students' attention.

The Beginning also has the **connection from the previous lesson**. This might be a simple review of what went on and perhaps a couple of simple questions given to students (selected because they should know the answers) around the room.

Now the important part; the **Lesson Aim(s)**, which should be succinct; the **Lesson Objectives** (few and simple) and the **Rationale** or the importance why they should all learn the lesson to the best of their ability.

For example, consider a lesson on electrical safety. It may start off like:

(Preparation of the chairs, AC, audio visual aids e.g. data projector, some equipment). The class is sitting down.

Draw the sketch (p.107) on the whiteboard (Wow! - got their attention).

"Good evening class, do you remember the last lesson on basic electrical components? What were some of the main components discussed? What is the function of a resistor? Which component is used in amplification?

Good! Well done!

Tonight, we are going to learn the main rules of electrical safety. (the Aim).

By the end of this lesson, you will be able to: recall the main rules of safety; relate the appropriate rule to situations commonly encountered; observe the main features of operation of some safety appliances; construct simple circuits to test aspects of safety; develop a positive belief in the need for safety in the workplace; and show initiative in applying safety procedures in new situations.
(the Objectives).

It is vital that you learn these rules and do not become complacent in your work. Remember the old saying: 'One flash and you're ash!' (Rationale).

So, let's begin the lesson."

2. **The middle** of the lesson contains the main teaching steps in sequence and with time allocations. These steps may vary from explanations and demonstrations by the teacher, student activities such as practical work, group discussions and private reading or notetaking. Each component of this part of the lesson should be a **logical sequence** to the next. It may be important for the teacher/instructor to assess each

major step with a few short questions and offer further explanation or re-teaching if it is obvious that a significant number of the class do not understand that section of work. The number of steps in this sequence should be kept to the minimum needed but this depends upon the attention span of the students. <u>Younger students with limited attention spans</u> (say 5-10 minutes) may need more simple steps than older students.

In lectures where the instructor's teaching takes up the main part of the lesson, this can be broken up into sections with questions to the class, use of audio-visual aids such as images or short videos. The continual drone of a boring lecturer using a single aid such as a PowerPoint presentation can be a disaster if the content of the presentation is simply read out to the students. This is called 'Death by PowerPoint' in the teaching profession as it kills attention and learning.

The dynamics of the class, or the difficulty of the topic may mean that not all of the middle part of the lesson is achieved. No problem, as this often happens, especially if a student introduces a topic worth exploring further with the entire class. The middle part of the lesson is then put aside and becomes the source of another lesson. Some of my best lessons have been student – generated enquiries on the topic planned. Careful about intended distractions!

For example, in the lesson on Electrical Safety, a student may bring up a concern about some specific detail which they had encountered in their daily work, such as the complication of a house having solar electrical panels. The lesson may then change to some specific details about applicable safety rules with solar-powered electrical systems.

3. **The end** is almost as important as the Beginning as it will round off the lesson and bring it to a logical end and it will also set the scene for the next lesson.

It may include a short test of the objectives, usually a few questions around the class or in a more formal session such as a separate training program may include a written test and perhaps a rating of the program.

Any homework or requirement for the next lesson would be included here. This may also include any remediation which might be needed in the next lesson. It is always a good idea for some homework to be given to Secondary students, even if it is a completion of a text-book summary or a few questions from the textbook.

What is vitally important over the whole lesson is **timing**. With experience, most teachers have a very good concept of how long parts of the lesson will take but if the lesson is varied in its presentation in the Middle section, then some allowance for it to be concluded satisfactorily with the End section. For this purpose, at least five minutes should be allowed at the end of the lesson time for such a logical conclusion and the connection to the next lesson so keep an eye on the time. A large clock at the back of the room is an advantage. It is totally unprofessional to be part way through a lesson and have students start to pack up or walk out because one has gone over time.

4.3 The prepared plan

Good teachers usually have their lessons thoroughly planned. Either on paper in a Teachers Diary or on their phone or tablet in a suitable folder. It is advisable that new teachers prepare their work in great detail and keep their prepared work in a strong cardboard folder, loose-leaf book or in specific folders on their portable electronic devices (with backups on their PC or on USB sticks).

With time and experience, after the particular lesson has been given several times, the amount of additional preparation and recording decreases to a few reminders in a diary with stored printed or electronic aids handy.

The 'Teachers Diary' often consists of open double pages which have places for the planning of the three steps of the lesson on the left-hand side and a page for notes on the right. A suggested (but here condensed) example for new teachers is given on the next page. In A4 format, such a template should be big enough to hold the entire lesson plan. A separate template is used for each new lesson and an example of a blank template which can be sized to order is given on the next page:

Lesson Title: _____

Week: _____   Date: __/____/_____
Day: _____   Lesson Times: _____

Preparation:

Motivation:

Previous Lesson:

Lesson Aim(s): _____
Objectives: _____
                           _____
                           _____
                           _____
                           _____
Rationale: _____

Lesson Steps:

Test of Objectives; Homework & Follow-Up:	Absentees:

This can be photocopied and enlarged to A4 size and used in a loose-leaf or arch folder as the left-hand side of a teaching book. Small teaching aids such as cardboard cut-outs, printed photos and the like can be stored in plastic sheet protectors and any electronic information can be held in small plastic protectors in separate USB drives.

As an example, consider the lesson previous discussed on Electrical Safety. This may be partly written up as:

(Not all of the lesson steps could be inserted here and this example has been greatly truncated)

Lesson Title:	*Introduction to Electrical Safety*

Week: 3	**Date:** 2 / 2 / 2020
Day: Monday	**Lesson Times:** 9:05 - 9:55

Preparation: Cartoon projected. Electrical meters. Circuit Kits.

Motivation: Trace sketch

Previous Lesson: Electrical components – resisters, transistors basic circuits.

Lesson Aim(s): to learn the main rules of electrical

Objectives: 1. recall the main rules of safety;
2. relate the appropriate rule to situations commonly encountered;
3. observe the main features of operation of some safety appliances;
4. construct simple circuits to test aspects of safety;
5. develop a positive belief in the need for safety in the workplace;
6. show initiative in applying safety procedures in new situations.

Rationale: Importance of daily safety in the workplace.

Lesson Steps:
1. Hand out component kits. Explain parts & use of each.
2. Explain task – Ex. 3.1-3, p. 34 of text.
3. Build each kit. Check student circuit.
4. Measure current flow and voltage across each component.
5. Students to short circuit where indicated. Check circuits.
6. Dismantle circuits. Restore/return kits.
7. Summary from questions.

Test of Objectives; Homework & Follow-Up: Quick questions. Copy P. 35 text as summary.	**Absentees:** Mr Bloggs.

So far, lesson planning has assumed that the lesson given is of the traditional teacher-centred type with students sitting at their desks with a teacher explanation and questions with possibly the use of textbooks, chalkboard/whiteboard, electronic media and with some sort of summary at the end.

Lesson preparation and planning will vary, especially in the Middle section, depending upon the type of lesson to be given. Some learning is more suited to the usual **teacher-centred approach** such as lectures, guest speaking programs, online and video lessons for remote education programs and other lessons of the student-centred type require different strategies which are more flexible but still require some teacher-directed pre-planning.

Demonstrations or 'show-and-tell (often with a guest teacher) are often an excellent teaching strategy to introduce a topic, show an object or process which is beyond the student's ability and range of skills or to reinforce current learning. Demonstrations are most effective if they:

- **work correctly** – a real problem with technical demonstrations, especially involving computers, is that they will not work or fail at the most critical moment (a corollary of Murphy's Law that 'anything that can go wrong will go wrong'). Practice the use of any technical equipment or sequence and rehearse the demonstration beforehand with duplicates if necessary. With computers, refresh caches and remove unwanted files; practice opening sequences; have log-in codes ready and find out how any failed program or App can be easily restored;

- **are kept short** – lengthy demonstrations, especially skills which are to be imitated by the students. If the skill is complex, it should be demonstrated first in its entirety and then broken down into separate parts which are then demonstrated again with the students imitating that part;

- **are given to all of the students** – this may mean re-arranging the class seating or having the group stand around at an appropriate distance (especially during live animal, chemistry or high-voltage electrical demonstrations!);

- **never explain and demonstrate at the same time.** Some demonstrations, especially those which may cause some excitement amongst the students, may require an explanation (or warning) before the demonstration. Others, especially those which are new and possibly highly motivational, can have the explanation after the excitement of the demonstration. Also keep any explanation short and in a good, audible voice;

- **slightly exaggerate** any movement. This will vary for each demonstration. If it is a body action, or the group is large, some exaggeration will aid in <u>all</u> students seeing the action as well as adding some drama or humour to the lesson;

- **avoid <u>unnecessary</u> movements** – especially if it is a requirement that students later imitate the movement. Also, it is important that the demonstration is given 'clean' that is without the demonstrator having to make unnecessary movements such as adjusting the light, getting more equipment and so on;

- **slow down complicated movements** – this is a learning experience, not slight-of-hand! These actions can also be repeated several times;

- **correct any mistakes made quickly and then give the correct demonstration.** Students will easily overlook a simple mistake but will imitate it if not corrected immediately; and

- **choose a good position for the demonstration.** The front of the classroom with students at an appropriate distance, sitting or standing will cover most simple demonstrations. Those requiring larger, exaggerated motion or the display of some large device should be given in a hall or outdoors in a safe location.

4.4 Types of lessons – student-centred approach.

Other learning situations are more appropriate to a **student-centred approach** such open lessons may include: enquiry-based practical lessons in science and workshops; student discussions and debates; group activities in the arts, sport and languages and so on.

Whilst the emphasis is on the student doing most of the work here, it is up to the teacher to quietly control the class, supply any appropriate items or equipment and then move around the group giving praise or remedial assistance as required. In group discussions, brief teacher intervention might be needed to spark some new discussion in a healthy direction or stop any discussion or outburst of a negative nature such as physical, gender, racial or religious abuse.

Consolidation, revision or study lessons can also be mainly student-based activities with the teacher providing the appropriate materials. These could be written exercises, educational games, computer simulations and exercises, textbook exercises, questionnaires, art works on special topics, constructed items or materials, preparation of student presentations or simply quite study. These can vary also in the level of student conversation and teacher interaction. Tutorials on past work are most useful for older students provided that they can work independently and cover the material set down for the time period. Younger students will need shorter periods of independent work interspaced with some teacher activity such as reviewing the exercises, marking questionnaires and tests, listening and critiquing student work.

4.5 Types of lessons – student-action approach.

Lesson planning also depends upon the type of student. For example, some students are kinaesthetic learners (who require movement to learn) or tactile learners (who require hands-on learning), traditional classroom environments can an obstacle to learning for these students. Opportunities should be provided so that such students can not only participate in the lesson, but also learn from it.

Kinaesthetic learners need to move their entire body and often just can't seem to sit still. They learn through their bodies and their sense of touch. It is not uncommon for such students to be 'diagnosed' by the traditional teacher as having Attention Deficit Disorder (ADD) or Attention-Deficit / Hyperactivity Disorder (ADHD). If a teacher suspects a student of possibly having these disorders then he/she should discuss this with experts and the student's parents.

Kinaesthetic learners also have excellent "physical" memory and they learn quickly and permanently by doing actions during their learning process. A lesson could make use of actions accompanying, words which the teacher first demonstrates, such as students remembering a phrase for the order of the planets:

(*All students stand up*:)

My: (Mercury) student points to themselves;
Very: (Venus)student shakes themselves arrogantly;
Elegant: (Earth) looking prim with nose in the air;
Mother: (Mars) shakes imaginary skirt;
Just: (Jupiter) holds up finger in the air with surprized look;
Sat: (Saturn) student goes to sits down;
Upon: (Uranus) looking about;
Nettles: (Neptune) all yell 'ouch!' and jump up!

There are many more learning situations where actions can be included such as in learning lists, relationships, stories and so on; almost every type of situation and learning can be dramatized. Exaggeration and practice are important.

Kinaesthetic learners are often gifted in physical activities like running, swimming, dancing, and other sports. They are typically very coordinated and have an excellent sense of their body in space and of body timing and have great hand-eye coordination. These features are often useful when 'volunteers' are called for in some classroom activity requiring good body skills. These students should be encouraged and their talents praised along with the academic achievements of their classmates.

Tactile learners learn through fine motor movements rather than whole body movement, being more moderate in their need for action than kinaesthetic learners.

Tactile learners learn primarily through the sense of touch through hand-on activities such as kit construction, use of technical instruments, building Lego technics kits, art works, workshop products, matching word cards and other games and performing other simple actions.

They also are best able to achieve and demonstrate their level of achievement through the use of projects where something needs to be assembled or even disassembled, say within a time limit. Homework projects are also good for such students.

Unfortunately, it should be remembered that kinaesthetic and tactile learners often have problems in restraining their movements and maintaining concentration. They tend to be easily distracted by their environment, have difficulty learning multiple steps and tend not to be good listeners. Special attention, rather than punishment, is appropriate once the student's needs have been identified.

In the lesson and preparation, care should be given to include such students within the lesson activities. This is not easy, but some of the activities previously mentioned goes down well with most students in the class and extra attention can be given whilst the others are involved in their own work.

4.6 Study and assignments

There may be a time when students will be given the chance to study for a test or simply to revise some aspect of work from a textbook or online source.

In traditional versions of such a lesson, students were forbidden to speak – 'silent study' was the term. This may be unreasonable in many circumstances as the student may wish to ask for help from a fellow student or from the teacher: the meaning of words, how to proceed and so on. A good general rule is that such study should be quiet, not silent, so that others are not disturbed with some movement permitted if students wish to consult a class library, computer or get some additional resource. The teacher should be active by moving around and assisting students with their work as well as watching out for lazy students who are doing very little (or playing computer/phone games).

There are some 'old fashioned' techniques that sometime get thrown out in the mad rush to 'go electronic'. Certainly, the uses of PCs, laptops and Tablets are to be encouraged as they can provide an instant connection with a (filtered) Internet or school-based network. However, there were some advantages of student note-taking in class and copying text and simple diagrams from the board or textbook. Large amounts of information, diagrams, photos and animations can be uploaded using the classroom WIFI for student records but there will be a time when the important parts of this information must be learnt for general use later or for assignments or for more immediate examinations.

Even with a wide range of electronic devices, memory games and the like, the practical use of old-fashioned skills of the chalkboard/whiteboard as well as the use of paper notebooks by the students are still valid. Considering some of the deficiencies of electronic information-gathering and the associated personal retention ability observed in the media, some of these older skills should be retained. Literacy levels tend to suffer as students get into the bad habit of using 'text-speak' as part of their normal communication. Spelling is also one concept which seems to have gone astray but should be retained. Especially when there is a concept that students should ignore grammar and spelling when trying to express themselves creatively. I would advocate that the spelling and grammar should be part of the creative writing process. One good but old-fashioned technique was to have the students correct any written spelling mistake and also write the misspelt word (correctly) in a reserved place in their notebook, diary or Tablet folder.

Terms such as 'lol' (laugh out loud), 'omg' (oh my god), pls (please) should be left to mobile (cell) phone texting and not for written or spoken English. The craze for shortening words, also derived from texting, is also changing how we speak – 'amaze' for 'amazing', 'totes' for totally, 'blates' for blatantly and so on do not fit in to an adult world which may require more 'higher-order' expression.

Having to write in a notebook assists in the later world which may require some penmanship when it comes to filling in reports, writing personal messages on cards or simply surviving in another world which may not require the use of electronic Word Processors.

Students once had pride in good hand-writing (need practice), reasonable grammar and spelling (<u>all teachers</u> should be good at this and teach it!), drawing skills (see a later chapter on this) and setting out their notes in a logical and systematic manner, often using colour. Marking student notebooks once a month seems to have gone out of the usual range of teaching duties, but it has great benefits for the communication skills of students. In addition, the **hand-eye coordination** required to copy down notes, diagrams etc. aids greatly to the mental ability of recall summaries and diagrams.

Allied to this is the other 'old fashioned' exercise which seems to have been lost is the use of repetition. Students once studied by:

- **summarizing** large amounts of text into short lists;

- **copying out diagrams** which show important processes;

- **making up mnemonics** to learn sequences; such as the one given earlier about the order of the planets from the Sun: <u>My Very Elegant Mother Just Sat Upon Nettles</u>. Other famous mnemonics include:

<u>How I Wish I Could Calculate Pi</u>. The number of letters gives the first seven digits of pi: 3.141592 but don't forget the decimal point!

<u>Dear Kate, Please Come Over For Great Spaghetti</u> for remembering the order of taxonomy in biology: Domain, Kingdom, Phylum, Class, Order, Family, Genus, Species;

<u>Every Good Boy Deserves Fun </u>for the order of the musical scale E,G,B,D,F; and

<u>Please Excuse My Dear Aunt Sally </u>for the order of mathematical operation as Parenthesis, Exponents, Multiplication, Division, Addition and Subtraction; and

- The use of funny sketches (my favourite with the class), especially in more difficult technical and poor memory sections.

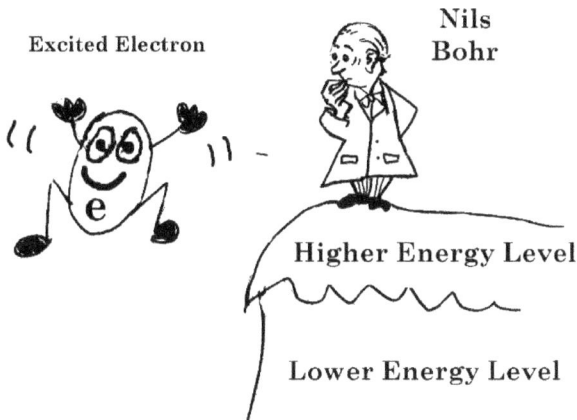

Excited Electron

Nils Bohr

Higher Energy Level

Lower Energy Level

A Quantum Leap

At home, study has to be:

- **in an ideal, quiet place** with good ventilation and lighting such as a good desk with a comfortable chair (not TOO cosy!) in a quiet room;

- **time consistent** – that is undertaken about the same time each day over a planned weekly schedule but with some flexibility for family time and leisure. Homework should be done ASAP before study as it has priority. My personal attitude was that often too much homework is given, often by several teachers in any one day. Often my homework consisted of finishing class summaries, some short reading of new text or watching or reviewing video clips from my intranet or the Internet;

- **self-motivated** without pressure to study, study, study etc. from parents. There must be a will to study for success (this may also come with an incentive!). There must be time (preferably straight after school) for play, socializing and relaxation;

- **active** with the student doing hand-eye or manipulative tasks rather than 'looking over' the work (at the football on TV beyond). A special problem occurs with students who try to learn by only re-reading their electronic uploads (little is 'downloaded' to their memory banks!);

- **varied** so that one does not get bored. Two or three different pieces of work per study session is better than several hours of the same thing. A study timetable of the week of is advisable excluding homework time but this must be flexible and not seen as an extension of school time schedules;

- **self-appraising** with the student setting some 'test' questions to answer later on;

- **may involve paired or group discussion** and study with questions being fired from members to each other. Networking is good for this if controlled;

- **preparation** of tasks such as giving an imaginary lesson – great for learning a subject;

- **construction** of an item, kit, artwork or shop product; and

- **rote learning** of phrases, definitions, lists, lines of plays etc. This might mean writing out the word, equation, phrase several times whilst speaking it out aloud. Old fashioned but it works!

Study and revision may also be entertaining and involve appropriate educational computer games and simulations which have to do with the topic. Even simple crosswords or find-the-word written games or word exercise are helpful, especially if the student is not keen on formal study (teachers can be sneaky!).

A good reference for doing assignments and study is:

Scott, W.J. 2016: *The Perfect Assignment.* Felix Publishing. info.felixpublishing@gmail.com

(A great little book which gets excellent results for school students and adults).

Of course, computer aids and educational games are now mainstream but their proper use must also be taught; even some teachers have a limited ability when it comes to producing documents, charts, lists as well as diagrams and graphs for electronic transfer and posting on school internal networks (intranets) or the Internet. Some teachers are also great at this and produce notes, interactive exercises, slide show presentations and videos which their students can access in class or at home on their PCs or laptops. For example, the following videos were used in my books and senior geology classes and are still currently online:

using a geology pick for prospecting (skill):
https://www.youtube.com/watch?v=VjQda-q1v1E

testing the cleavage of minerals:
https://www.youtube.com/watch?v=_RwRQ3Cgn
fg

or going underground in a virtual excursion:
https://www.youtube.com/watch?v=OCbccRGRh
84&feature=youtu.be

(you might like to view my other world excursions to the Amazon, Antarctica, sailing windjammers, climbing glaciers and others by clicking on to my face on that page then looking for the rest)

Students now are able to produce rather sophisticated assignments using a great variety of multimedia. It becomes an additional task for teachers to grade these assignments, especially when it comes to assessing the ownership of parts or all of such assignments. There are computer programs to assist in such assessment and in time just ordinary experience which helps in locating plagiarized work.

Be like a Scout – always be prepared. Teaching is never predictable!

4.7 So now what?

For the First-year-out teacher or the instructor new to a training institution or organisation, it is important to build on the knowledge and skills of lesson preparation initially learned.

Preparing and planning for new lessons as suggested in this chapter can be an intensive and very time-consuming operation. Once the neophyte teacher/instructor has survived their first year or so and has a good collection of lesson plans and associated teaching aids, then this intensity can be relaxed a little and more time spent in developing other skills of teaching and becoming more involved in some of the other aspects of education and the life of the school or institution…and perhaps having more of a private life of their own.

It is recommended that lesson plans once prepared and used should be kept for the next cycle of similar lessons. Naturally there may have to be some modification for future lessons as teaching is never static but changes with the type of classes and their needs.

An organised folder for any paper lesson plans or a decent-sized portable hard-drive for any electronic plans and teaching aids should be maintained.

A filing cabinet or box would be suitable for teaching aids such as cut-outs, overhead transparencies, 35 mm slide sets, magnetic strips, photographs, maps, charts, master copies for printed notes, small items of interest etc. Today, with electronic media being a main part of teaching and instruction, storage can be simpler by using portable hard drives (say, 1 terabyte). A wide range of items can now be stored and carried from class to class. These would include abbreviated lesson plans/teachers' diary, collections of photos, audio clips and video clips with which the lesson can be augmented. It still might be more convenient for the teacher to have a paper Teachers Diary in which the daily reminders and in-class notations are made.

As time progresses, the now experienced teacher/instructor would have given lessons many times over and the parts of each lesson would become almost a well-rehearsed script. Only the new variations for each lesson and collection of teaching aids need be taken into the classroom.

However, there may be occasions when even the experienced teacher may need to revert to the classical, full-scale preparation of a lesson. This may occur when they are:

- giving a demonstration lesson to visiting student teachers;

- as part of an institution 'Open Day';

- having their own teaching assessed by a supervisor;

- encountering a totally new topic due to a syllabus change; or

- preparing supportive material for new colleagues.

An experienced teacher/instructor with a good extensive education and personal experience of life should find that giving an impromptu lesson to a new group of students is not as difficult as it was in the early days of their profession. Good teachers become good actors and every classroom is a new stage.

Chapter Five

Out and About – Excursions and Visits

5.1 The need to go places.

Sometimes there is a need to take the class out of the comfort zone of the institution and into the wider world. It is always an exciting time regardless of the age of the student. Adults seem to enjoy a 'day out' just as much as young children. The problem for them is that they are expected to learn during this event. For the teacher, it will be a day (or night) of anxiety and constant vigilance.

Some outings are taken simply as an additional part of the incidental learning which goes on regardless of the teacher's efforts. These visits may be to the theatre, a museum or some other cultural zone with the broad aim of improving the students' general appreciation of some of the better things in life.

At other times the visit may be more specifically planned as part of the wider curriculum which may make such visits mandatory and assessable. These may also include museum visits of an artistic, natural, scientific or historical nature and the students are then expected to be involved in some set of activities for an assignment, talk or general discussion.

Excursions could include such other places as a(n):

- factory to learn about production of important items;

- farm to see how animals and crops are raised;

- national park to learn about the natural world;

- scientific laboratory to look at technical issues;

- art gallery to see how paintings and sculptures are made and sold;

- stock exchange and other places of business;

- mine site to see how minerals or fuels are obtained;

- specific environment such as a marine rock platform, rain forest or cave complex; or

- other local site worth first-hand investigation which cannot be simulated in the classroom,

There may be some brave souls who will undertake excursions which go further afield and take a great deal longer. They may last from a simple weekend away to a local camp or tourist resort for some sporting or environmental study or it may mean an extended trip overseas for broadening the students' understanding of foreign languages and customs. Some schools and youth organisations offer specific field adventure programs which may be run as a school activity. As a teacher, I have organised snow-skiing trips, caving expeditions and 'tall ship' training of up to a week in duration, not to mention annual camps with school military cadets. One never knows the direction and places a teaching career will go.

Regardless of the type or duration of the excursion, preparation and planning is usually much more detailed and intense as they require constant 24-hour supervision and responsibility of the student. Some assistance can be had by having several other teachers and parents involved, but the responsibility still remains with the organiser.

5.2 Preparation and Planning

Basically, there are three parts to any excursion or field trip:

1. preparation for the trip;

2. taking the excursion; and

3. following it up.

Naturally each section will vary in its intensity and requirements depending upon the nature of the trip and that of the students going on it. An international excursion lasting several weeks will require much more effort than a simple part-day field trip. The ages. Gender and typical group behaviour of the students will determine a wide range of factors such as basic living requirements, type of supervision, transportation requirements, costs and so on. Students with special needs will also introduce another factor in preparation and execution of the trip.

A simple day excursion would probably begin with a teacher reconnaissance of the area or contact with the organisation which will be visited. Many organisations such as museums, art galleries, large libraries, theatres, some factories, national parks and scientific bodies usually have Public Relations people who are happy to do most of the internal organisation and may even have appropriate assignment guides or work sheets for different levels of students. Many unfortunately do not and it will be up to the teacher to prepare these guidelines and work sheets based on their prior visits and knowledge of the venue.

Preparation for day excursions usually requires:

1. **permission and justification** for the excursion with one's superiors. Sometimes certain excursions are mandated by the syllabus or deemed 'highly desirable' by the school or institution. The need for the excursion and an outline plan must be discussed with one's superiors before further planning;

2. **teacher reconnaissance of the area** – this is always a good idea even if the area is well-known as conditions change. There is nothing like arriving at an environmental site to find it overgrown with concrete!

3. **review of latest information** – this might be tide charts for a coastal excursion which must be done safely at low tide; opening hours and parking facilities for museums and other institutions; any safety rules and preparation required by the organisation being visited such as a mine site or national park and so on;

4. **organisation of transport, accommodation** and other external arrangements will be required well in advance. This and any entry fee will determine the basic cost for each student or the school administration. The use of public transportation may also be a consideration if the visit is relatively local and then other factors such as timetables, location of pick up and set down points and general behaviour are factors. In most cases it is easier to hire a bus;

5. **acquisition of additional staff** and parents may require further reorganisation of school schedules and a considerable amount of personal effort with one's colleagues. Some excursions naturally are more attractive than others and these usually have plenty of volunteers;

6. **internal organisation** involves basic preparation and planning with aims, objectives and rationale clearly defined; sequential steps of the excursion; equipment needed such as a First Aid kit (and someone who can use it!); communication plan and/or equipment; and most importantly, a good class roll of students attending.

An Excursion Guide should be sent home to parents and a Permission Form should be required in reply. These forms are more for information rather than legal documents and an example of each is given on the next two pages.

Note: Such Consent Forms <u>DO NOT absolve the teacher and guides of any moral and legal responsibility</u> and should not imply any legal responsibility other than that of the organizing teacher and their institution. Consent Forms merely provides f e e d b a c k f r o m t h e parents or guardian acknowledging their understanding of the details of the excursion. Beware of faked Consent Forms, especially from students known to have difficult backgrounds;

<insert institution letter head>
EXCURSION DETAILS

DATE: <insert date and times>   **CLASS:** < insert class/group>

DESTINATION: <insert location/name of place or organisation>
This excursion is an integral part of the semester's programme.   All students will be required to complete an assignment, associated with the excursion, which will contribute towards the assessment of the subject.

ARRANGEMENTS: < insert details of transportation, time of departure and return etc.>
The bus will leave at___< time>___ and returns at___< time> approx.
(Bus company can be contacted at: **<name and contact number>**
Students are to meet at: **< meeting place and time>** but are not to enter the bus until directed to do so. The normal rules of the Institution apply at all times.

COST:

STAFF GOING on the excursion will be: < name(s) of staff and contact numbers >

SPECIAL REQUIREMENTS: < special requirements such as allergies, diets as well as expectations about dress, personal items such as cameras, mobile phones, writing material, safety precautions etc. Also, any special rules of behaviour and group actions if lost etc.>

Yours faithfully,

< name of person in authority>   Contact number_**< insert >**

Figure 5.1 A simple Excursion Guide

<insert institution letter head>
EXCURSION CONSENT FORM

DATE: <insert date and times>   CLASS: < insert class/group>

DESTINATION: <insert location/name of place or organisation>

CONSENT FORM: Please return to supervising teacher by:
< insert time/date>
I have read the above information and agree for...... <insert student
name>..................to go on the excursion.

Special information concerning my daughter's/son's welfare
that the supervising staff should know is as follows:

<insert special requirements such as allergies, dietary
requirements, medical conditions etc.>

Phone contact of parent/guardian:
Home: ....Work.............................

Signature: .... (Parent/Guardian)

Date: ....

Figure 5.2: A typical Consent Form

and

7. provision should be made for any student who
cannot attend the excursion but will be at the
school. School-age students should be allocated

to a similar class for the day and adult students would need to find their own alternatives. Both groups would be expected to find out about the information that would be learnt during the visit;

During the excursion:

1. **extra vigilance** by the teachers would be required and this also would depend on the location of the excursion. This is very important if students must negotiate dangerous places such as roads, railway lines, factory floors, mine sites and the like;

2. **larger classes** may be broken up into smaller groups under the supervision of a teacher with perhaps a parent or two in support. Parents who go on excursions should not be expected to take on the responsibility of a teacher, nor do they have the legal status to do so. They are there to assist only;

3. **provide for emergencies** such as having a First Aid Kit, being trained in First Aid and taking charge of student health devices such as inhalers and other medication with a list of ownership of

each etc. Other provisions may include carrying extra food (such as glucose lollies) and water;

4. **controlling use of student equipment** such as when mobile (cell) phones can be used. If the institution has a 'no phone' policy in the classroom, there may be a consideration for students to take their phones in case they become separated from the group, but use of the phones socially would be forbidden and they should be turned off during the trip. The leading teacher of each group should have an active phone with a well-charged battery. Portable radio devices should be banned although there may be some flexibility with the use of these with earphones on long bus/train trips;

5. **obeying the instructions of local guides** who may be taking the group around their institution, mine or outdoor area is paramount. The use of local guides DOES NOT absolve teacher responsibility, but rather adds another level of group control;

6. **NEVER put students at risk** by taking them into known areas of danger. Some excursions such as hiking, rope work, skiing, caving and sailing might 'push the envelope' but in these

situations, the teacher(s) must be trained in such activities and the best safety equipment be provided and checked for each student. Prior approval for such activities must be obtained both from the school/institution and parents. Students who find that they cannot participate in such activities should NOT be forced into them but given alternative supervision;

7. **ensure good communications** both within the group and with outside authorities. Mobile (cell) phones are very useful for the supervising teacher on any excursion but only if they work. The remoteness of an area may mean the use of an appropriate two-way radio, but these have their limits, especially in their range. If a bus is being used for transportation, these often have longer-range two-way radio and any park rangers or guides should also have good communication. Check communications before the excursion by either personal reconnaissance or finding out such information from locals; and

8. **always be aware of the number** of students in the group and their behaviour, especially in more difficult locations. This is especially true for students with known behavioural problems. They might be assigned in 'special role' to assist

the teacher in some manner. Counting students at each leg of the trip and especially in the transport on the way home is essential. If a student is lost then a search may be needed whilst the others stay in a supervised group. Each student should be aware of the group's 'action if lost' plan. This will probably suggest staying put or moving in an obvious direction to a road or tree line which would be across the line of walking but it should be simple and easy to do.

Additional help may be required by members of the institution being visited or by the appropriate authorities but TIME is the most important factor. If groups are going into remote areas, such as hiking in national parks, then it is important that the group stay together; a 'buddy system' may be appropriate so that students also watch out for 'wanderers'. Also, appropriate emergency equipment such as extra food and water and shelter such as thermal blankets should be carried by each student if possible. The appropriate authorities or local police should be notified in advance with a 'time after' when a rescue may be needed. It is vital that these authorities also be notified as the trip finishes and all students and staff have been checked.

Follow up the visit or excursion by:

1. **revising the excursion** in the first opportunity. This should involve active student participation such as: questions from the class as well as from the teacher; re-visiting the excursion using video or photographs, Internet satellite images or the institutions Home Page; revision of requirements and preparation of student work sheets or assignments;

2. **collecting any student work-sheet** or assignment on the trip after an appropriate preparation time and the marking or grading of the assignments;

3. **discussion** on any work sheets or assignments and answers to questions with further review of the excursion;

4. **other specific follow-up lessons** on any aspect of the excursion e.g. a trip to an Art Gallery may then be followed by some student art work based on the style seen at the gallery such as an Impressionist work. A visit to an environmental

park or agency could also spark further environmental activities at the school or institution; and

5. **providing feedback to parents** such as a formal 'thank you' to those involved and a summary sheet to all parents about the activities of the excursion.

It is usual also for the supervising teacher to provide their superiors with a report on the excursion showing the positive and negative outcomes with plans for improvement. The organisation of the entire excursion, along with this report and appropriate contact people and their telephone numbers should be filed by the supervising teacher in an appropriate records section so that other teachers can use it for later excursions.

5.3 Longer excursions

Trips requiring overnight accommodation and extensive travel will naturally require a considerable amount of preparation well in advance as well as additional supervision during the trip. It is most helpful if a visit to another location also involves a 'companion' institution at this location. This adds to the supervisory security as well as some assistance with organisation at the site and with transport and accommodation. Such visits, especially in overseas locations are the best way to go on such excursions to do with the learning of new language, culture and geography. On a separate issue, it may be an advantage for the entire school/institution administration to have an 'exchange' system with some companion school interstate or overseas.

Camping trips in outdoor areas or in formal camps require the organiser and any camp or park official to be fully knowledgeable about the nature of the students and what is required for their learning activities. A simple camping trip using only the teaching staff and students must consider the preparation and limitations of the students. Some students have no idea whatsoever in living in the field and so comprehensive prior training may be needed. This might be a mock-up of the camp at the school include: the erection and use of tents (preferably light weight two-man types); cooking equipment, especially if local fire bans are in place; sleeping bags and their types; clothing appropriate to the climate and especially the use of wet weather protection; water and food provisions, especially the need for light weight foods; the need for a good, well-supported and comfortable pack; and any navigation equipment such as GPS units, maps and compass and how to use them.

A good ready reference for use of equipment and emergencies as well as a light weight First Aid kit should be carried by at least the supervising teacher. A good reference for outdoor activities is my book based on many years of taking such excursions:

Scott, Dr. Peter T., 2020: **A Pocketbook for Hiking and Survival.**
(Felix Publishing info.felixpublishing@gmail.com)

Overseas visits can also best be facilitated by making use of a 'companion' school or by arranging it formally with educational bodies who promote such trips. Some useful information can be found at:

https://www.google.com/url?sa=t&rct=j&q=&esrc=s&source=web&cd=&cad=rja&uact=8&ved=2ahU KEwiHivzeuavtAhVGzjgGHUYsChwQFjABegQI ARAC&url=https%3A%2F%2Fwww.education.ac t.gov.au%2F__data%2Fassets%2Fword_doc%2F00 09%2F1043469%2FOverseas-Excursions-Manual-

23-November-2016.docx&usg=AOvVaw2jtllnRnd-v0MidoU5zhgg
(cut and paste this URL if no direct link possible)

https://www.education.vic.gov.au/Documents/school/principals/management/oslearnexpresource.pdf

https://www2.education.vic.gov.au/pal/excursions/guidance/overseas-travel

https://www.internationalaffairs.org.au/youth-and-community/study-tours/

https://www.study.vic.gov.au/Shared%20Documents/en/Sister-Schools/Sister-schools-resource-kit.pdf

https://ro.uow.edu.au/cgi/viewcontent.cgi?referer=https://www.google.com/&httpsredir=1&article=1307&context=jutlp

http://www.iier.org.au/iier27/hains-wesson-2.pdf

Some of the needs or problems with organising a private school/institution overseas involves:

1. **need for good travel advice** about the country – some personal experience about the 'fine detail' may be needed which can come from own or reliable private sources e.g. watch out for illicit 'taxis' in some countries which are into kidnapping. For some remote advice see:

   https://www.smartraveller.gov.au/destinations

2. **passports, visas and vaccinations** required for each student, some of whom may have some travel problems with going to a country or some medical issues;

3. **language issues** when the country's language is not the same as the home school/institution. It would be hoped that someone doing the organisation would have the appropriate language at the local level (rather than just having done a brief online course!). Even students well-trained in a Language Class will have difficulties with the speed of the local language and any local dialect difference. Students should at least have some courtesy phrases and some concept of cultural differences as overseas inhabitants often have different views of student behaviour and culture. Some of the basics should include:

LANGUAGE	TERMS (my apologies to native speakers)		
English	Please	Thank You	Sorry
Chinese	请 Qǐng [shing]	谢谢 Xièxiè [shersheh]	抱歉 Bàoqiàn [bow cherh]
Japanese	お願いします Onegaishimasu [on egai sh mas]	ありがとう Arigatō [ari gat oh]	ソリー Sorī [sori eh]
Spanish	por favor [por favore]	gracias [gracias]	lo siento [lo see ento]
French	s'il vous plaît [sil vu play]	merci [mehr see]	Pardon [par don]
Italian	per favore [per favoray]	Grazie [graht see]	Scusa [(e)scuzah]
German	Bitte [bitterh]	Vielen Dank [feellen dunk]	Es tut uns leid [es toot en slide]

Figure 5.3: Some foreign courtesy terms

4. packing issues such as over-packing and packing banned items (especially for airlines). Students should be given some additional assistance in what and how to pack, especially in the items not allowed by Customs. Also, the choice of travel bags and what can go as 'hand-luggage'. This MUST be done carefully as Customs agents are usually unforgiving! A list of what is allowed plus some hints on light-weight travelling is useful. Don't expect parents to have this information, so advise them and get them to check. For brief visits, a small 'cabin bag' may be all that is needed but check weight and size requirements. Larger bags should also be kept down in size and should have a good set of wheels and carrying handle. Luggage tags should be on all bags with the name of the school, as well as inside the bags as proof of ownership;

5. **travel bookings** should be kept to the experts so use Travel Agents who are used to group bookings. Some research may be needed here unless the school/institution has a preferred agent. Consider the major mode of transport (aircraft, train, ship) and the need for students to be together. Organise students in pairs or small groups who will be near each other and who are charged with mutual protection and conduct. Also consider connections and transfers between major transport. Allow extra time at stations or airports and limit movement at these places. Be aware of time differences and make it a point to remind students to reset watches. Also consider the transportation needed to get to the airport, station of wharf and also transportation

on arrival to get to the final destination. Set times with wide margins if parents are dropping their student off at the meeting place at the start of the journey and describe a prominent meeting area. Control is vital and likely to cause some teacher concern, so also delegate authority and take some time out if possible;

6. **travelling problems** such as travel sickness, poor behaviour, excessive movement over excitement (common) and wandering will need to be controlled by the teachers with the help of travel guides or transport staff.

7. **onsite control is important**. Restrict movement at any accommodation, especially hotels by alerting their staff to such limitations. Having teaching staff accommodated near groups of students (say on the same floor etc) is an advantage but needs prior organisation with the management. Many hotels and resorts welcome emails to this effect so that they know of what to expect and what they can do to try to help;

8. **movement in foreign localities** is best done as organised 'group tours', but if on foot or taking local transport, be aware of dangerous places, local habits and how local transport systems

operates including current fares – cost and how paid. Pair students up for mutual protection;

9. **have an 'if lost' plan** by keeping movement down to a minimum, maintaining tight group control and having each student made aware of the locality and where to go if separated from the group; and

10. **have active work** for the students such as a guide book with questions or specific things to do at each location.

5.4 Some legal aspects of excursions.

Most teachers will take all appropriate care of their students during an excursion. The law can be very specific but often operates on precedent and is subject to change. This section is based on my studies in Educational Law at the Master's level in Australia in the late 1990's, so watch out laws change!

There was a time when teachers were considered as being *in loco parentis* meaning that they had the same responsibility as a normal parent (although some would say that this Latin means that 'parents are crazy'. wrong!). To have the responsibility suited to a classroom of 30 to 40 students of different and often unknown behaviours and personalities, would drive the average parent crazy. Those attempting 'home schooling' are well aware of this! In general. The law requests that teachers owe a responsibility to not only give all due care to the student or group of student but also be able to foresee any potential problem which might cause injury or affront to any student. This is the concept of 'reasonable foreseeability' (the case of *Donoghue V Stevenson, 1932*).

The other main issue is that of Duty of Care. If any problem arises, it must be shown that:

- the individual or institution **had a duty of care** towards the student(s); and that

- this **duty had either not been taken, foreseen or had failed in some way**.

On an excursion, it is very obvious that there is a duty of care to each student and it also must be shown that this duty was breeched by the teacher involved (*Geyer V Downs, 1977*).

Whilst some argue that, once students have been given over to an expert guide in a safe environment, their duty of care is now transferred (see Barrell, G.R. & Partington, J.A. 1985: *Teachers and the Law*. 6th Edit. Cambridge University Press p. 485), I do not think that such complacency is worth the risk and that the teacher should continue exercising their duty of care. If there seems to be any conflict between the teacher and guide, then any risks should be pointed out. Not all guides are in full understanding of the group dynamics of an institution's students.

The other factor is that it must also be proven by the plaintiff (the adult student or 'their next best friend' if a child) that the teacher failed to foresee a problem or that they generally failed in their duty of care.

This concept of 'reasonable foreseeability' is why teachers now have to consider Workplace Health and Safety issues for every school-based activity and provide a written analysis of such issues before each lesson. A typical WH & S analysis is given in Figure 5.3.

< Institution name and letterhead>
Risk Assessment Form

Date: _____ Class: _____

Location: _____

Lesson Name/Type: _____

Teacher-in-charge: _____

ACTIVITY	RISK* LEVEL	RISK	PREVENTATIVE ACTION
< add rows depending upon number of risks>			

* Level as L=low, M=medium, H=high

FIRST AID & OTHER SAFETY EQUIPMENT:

TEACHER TRAINED IN:

STUDENT SPECIAL NEEDS:

TRANSPORT/TRAVEL RISKS:

OTHER:

Figure 5.3: A simplified WH & S Risk Assessment form

More detailed information and analysis guides can be found at:

https://education.qld.gov.au/initiatives-and-strategies/health-and-wellbeing/workplaces/safety/managing/risk-management

https://www.education.vic.gov.au/school/teachers/studentmanagement/excursions/Pages/outdoorrisk.aspx

https://www.owfc.com.au/Childcare.asp?_=Excursion%20Risk%20Assessment

https://www.google.com/url?sa=t&rct=j&q=&esrc=s&source=web&cd=&cad=rja&uact=8&ved=2ahUKEwi84cHf1KvtAhXiyDgGHQchBdsQFjACegQIBxAC&url=https%3A%2F%2Fapp.education.nsw.gov.au%2Fsport%2FFile%2F1419&usg=AOvVaw0YkSV0qKL5ogULMhE4tWTl
(cut and paste this URL or use key words to search)

https://www.aisnsw.edu.au/Resources/WAL%204%20[Open%20Access]/Science%20and%20Technology%20Risk%20Assessment%20Guidelines.pdf#%5B%7B%22num%22%3A50%2C%22gen%22%3A0

%7D%2C%7B%22name%22%3A%22XYZ%22%7D
%2C69%2C517%2C0%5D

(cut and paste this URL or use key words to search
for APPENDIX A)

Chapter Six

Lights, Action Camera.... Teaching Aids

In case of
POWER FAILURE
Break Glass

6.1 Introduction

A teaching/training aid is any item or system which can be used to compliment teaching. It is not meant to replace the skills of teaching but may be used for motivation, enhancing the learning or to illustrate, simulate or demonstrate some situation, process or environment which cannot be done within the classroom.

Teaching aids have been used since teaching began and in more modern times have included:

- chalkboards;

- whiteboards;

- felt boards (blanket boards);

- notice boards;

- charts and maps;

- models and dioramas;

- small items of interest;

- printed handout material;

- photographs, photographic slides and strips;

- overhead projectors;

- episcopes (projects images of solid objects such as live specimen), microprojectors (microscopes with camera) and video cameras;

- radio, records, audio tapes and music files;

- movie projectors and video (data) projectors;

- television, videos and video files;

- computer games and simulations; and

- smart touch screen computers.

6.2 Features of good teaching aids

The basic concepts are that teaching/training aids should be:

- applicable to the teaching content and skills;

- pitched at a level the class can understand;

- clear and easy to understand;

- useable within the teaching area;

- be suitable without offensive content;

- easy to set up and use (usually before the lesson); and

- used as required and over a short time (unless a feature film or video).

It is strongly recommended that any complex aid, especially electronic or those requiring some construction, should be tested beforehand and their use practiced. This also allows for a preview of the content in case that it may have gender, racial or other unpleasant sections.

6.3 Use of teaching aids

Teaching/training aids can be used for:

- **motivation and introduction of new work.** Hopefully it will have some bearing on the new work but it may just be a small item to start some interest;

- **reinforcement of teaching objectives.** The aid may be used at the start of the lesson or as the appropriate step of the lesson has been reached. It may be used to build up the content of the lesson e.g. use of diagrams on a whiteboard;

- **presentation of items or situations outside of the classroom** such as environments, processes and skills. It may include a short video or audio clip from a guest speaker;

- **simulations** of different processes to show how they work. This could be structured as a 'real-life' simulation, such as landing a lunar lander on the Moon or an animated flow diagram;

- **magnification** of small objects such as in using a video camera coupled to a microscope or telescope and used with a wide-screen data-projector; and

- **recording of excursions** or rare in-class demonstrations. These are idea for revision lessons.

6.4 Chalkboards, whiteboards and felt boards

Chalkboards have been around for centuries and were originally constructed of slate. These days they are often a material such as wood painted with matte black, green or dark blue paint. Unfortunately, many teacher-training institutions neglect to train their students on how to use this most basic teaching aid.

'Chalk' comes in compressed sticks of calcium carbonate (the original chalk) or calcium sulfate ('plaster of Paris') or barium sulfate ('dustless chalk'). Usually, a teacher will break a long stick in half to stop it breaking when writing on the board. They give a good surface contact and come in many colours including black, with white or yellow being the preferred common-use colour. Chalk can be very dusty and in earlier times, teachers could be easily identified by their white dust-covered clothing. None of the 'chalks' are toxic but excessive dust can cause some irritation to the eyes and lungs as well as drying out the skin.

Whiteboards became popular from about the 1960's, especially in corporate boardrooms and in the military. The best consists of a plastic (layered or painted) coating over a thin sheet of steel which makes them ideal for attaching painted or printed words, diagrams, photographs etc. which have had magnetic strips pasted onto them.

In schools, this magnetic facility is usually unknown or not used by teachers. Whiteboard marker pens are used as the writing/drawing implement and these may contain toxic solvents such as alcohols and ketones, some of which can be absorbed through the skin. They can cause skin and eye irritation over time.

Teachers and students sometimes mistake the usual 'felt pens' for whiteboard markers and use them to write on the whiteboard. These are permanent ink pens (and are often labelled as such) and so do not erase off the board with the usual eraser. If this occurs, use a rag lightly covered in alcohol to remove the marks and then dry the board. There are several types of whiteboard cleaning sprays which also do the job, but I have found them to be irritating to the lungs.

If a whiteboard exists in your teaching room, test its ability to hold a magnet by using a 'fridge magnet'. If it attaches to the surface, then a whole new range of teaching strategies can now take place.

Use coloured or white cardboard with felt pens to make words, letters, diagrams, or use photographs. Paste magnetic strips (save old fridge calendars and cut them up to about 4 cm x 2 cm) onto the backs of the cards made using adhesive tape. The cards can now be put onto the whiteboard as:

- sequences of letters to spell words;

- sequences of words to spell sentences;

- list of words in order or not;

- sections of flow diagrams showing processes;

- parts of diagrams to be reassembled on the board;

- positions of players on a sports field which can be moved about;

- parts of machinery and devices which can have parts which can be moved; and even

- overlays of cross-sections e.g. the interior of the Earth covered with the usual surface photograph.

Students are often fascinated when this system is used, especially if the teacher throws the magnetised word or diagram onto the board from a distance (also a good student game by throwing magnetic shapes or words onto a target or chart). Words or diagrams can then be joined using lines or curved using a marker pen. In this way, complex diagrams can be built up for student summaries at the end of the lesson.

Felt boards (blanket boards) are a cruder form of teaching board more commonly used in camps and outdoors where there are no teaching facilities. A woollen blanket straight off a bed and hung over a vertical flat surface such as a cupboard or fence will do the job. Words, diagrams, charts and the like must be prepared in advance and large pieces of coarse sandpaper stuck to their reverse side. These will then stick onto the woollen surface of the 'board'.

6.5 More on chalkboards

Chalkboards seemed to have become obsolete in some schools but are still widely used, especially in schools where funding prevents the installation of whiteboards. Chalkboards are very versatile and can be used in many different ways unknown to most teachers. Some little 'tricks of the trade' include:

- **drawing a complex image** or cartoon onto the board by projecting and tracing it using a dark pencil (say a 2B). This trace can be projected using an overhead projector (and transparency traced off the original or photocopied), slide projector (by cutting out the cartoon, mounting it in a slide mount and then painting it with cooking oil to make it transparent) or direct from a data projector connected to a computer.

With the trace on the board and unseen by the students, the 'expert artist' teacher simply follows the trace with chalk. Instant professional image or cartoon. Great motivation at the start of the lesson.

This can also be used for teachers who have difficulty writing in horizontal lines. A ruler and dark pencil can be used to draw guiding lines across the board;

- **making a two-layered image** which can have the outer covering 'cut away' by simply erasing it. This is done by drawing the lower image in **wet** chalk and allowing it to dry before covering it with the 'surface' of dry chalk. When erased, only the dry chalk surface comes off, exposing the layer below. Good for doing cross-sections of machinery, buildings, geological beds etc. At the end, the lower layer will need to be washed off with a damp rag;

- **seal a good diagram** for permanent use such as a graph axes, map outline or other re-useable diagram using a sugar spray (1 teaspoon / 250 ml) which makes it 'permanent'. When dry, this can be written upon with dry chalk which can also be erased. Remove the original diagram by using a damp rag;

- **making perfect dotted lines** is done by holding a good length of chalk (usually the thicker half) at almost right-angles to the board and then lightly dragging it across the surface. With practice, a perfect dotted line is formed. Students are most impressed with this.

If the chalkboard is new or shiny, use the flat of a whole stick and completely cover the board in chalk. This is then erased off using the proper eraser or soft cloth.

If the board is very dirty from poor use of the eraser over time, wipe it over with a damp cloth and then treat it as a new board.

Leave re-painting of boards to the experts. However, the teacher can make a small board for excursion use by painting a small (say 100 cm x 40 cm) board with blackboard paint (from a hardware store) and then mounting it in a strong frame with a carry handle on top. A cork pin board could then be glued to the reverse side for notices.

When using a chalkboard, some basic rules apply:

- **position the board** to your left-hand side if you are right-handed (and vice versa) and don't stand in front of it when finished;

- **do NOT talk and write** on the board at the same time. Talk to the students and not the board;

- **face the board squarely** when writing – this will ensure a better chance of writing horizontally;

- **use the eraser with a downward motion** – this will prevent causing too much dust to fly;

- **avoid squeaking chalk** by breaking a single stick in half and using its rough end;

- **don't clutter the board**. Like most documents, clutter makes reading difficult so space out the work and don't fill up the entire board with writing. Keep information brief, practice drawings beforehand;

- **always remove unwanted material** but give the students time to view or copy what has been written. When entering the room, erase any old material left by the previous teacher;

- **erase the board before leaving** and ensure that an eraser and chalk are left for the next person. Many teachers carry their own box of different-coloured chalk and their own (labelled) eraser; and

- **use a 'pointer'** for emphasis on sections of the board. A small telescopic pointer with a red tip, which fits into the pocket is a good idea or even a pen-shaped laser pointer. In the 'old days' cane pointers were used for other effects such as discipline (not on!).

6.6 Evaluating written text

When it comes to using textbooks, guide books and other written material, the teacher/instructor should ensure that the written material is not only culturally and socially acceptable but is at a reading level appropriate to the age of the student. This is very important with the early years of Primary Education when young students are at the beginning stages of language development. It may also apply to material used with students with lower reading skills and with those new arrivals who have English only as a second language.

When considering the readability of any material given out to the students of a particular age, one must consider the:

- length of the words – long words often confuse;

- length of the sentence and paragraph – long sentences are often boring and convey too much information for the student to absorb. This also applies to paragraphs;

- use of technical terms – which may be common place to the scientist, engineer, mathematician or other expert, but may be out of the vocabulary range of the student;

- use of foreign words or phrases which may be de rigueur for some aficionados and delivered ad nauseam as a fait accompli en masse to the class is not advisable. This usually ends up making the teacher persona non grata. So, caveat emptor! (whatever all of that means!);

- use of space; or lack of it. No one gets interest out of a text, webpage or large set of notes which reads like an old-fashioned telephone book. The use of open space, simple paragraphs, diagrams and photographs help to complement the written text, makes it easier to read and remember and makes it more enjoyable; and

- the excessive use of diagrams, drawings and other graphics etc. with minimal written text for older students is colourful but probably lacks sufficient information. This does NOT apply to younger students or students with limited reading ability where such illustrations help to tell the story and explain the meaning of words, concepts and emotions. I have reservations about the extensive use of so-called 'Adult Graphic Novels' which seem to have become popular amongst teens and adults in place of more traditional literature. These graphic novels require limited reading ability and little imagination from their readers.

When a teacher is in doubt about the 'readability' of a proposed student textbook, assigned novel or even a webpage, they could do their own analysis of the work by taking random samples of text throughout the work and then using one of several different 'Readability Scales'. Some of these can be found at:

https://www.litinfocus.com/5-accurate-methods-for-measuring-text-readability/

http://smdcourse.sjtu.edu.cn/_tank_/f/course/20170417/69c13efca22d665d6e56e5de0b94ef56/Measurement%20of%20Readability.pdf

https://blog.ung.edu/press/measure-readability/

http://www.standards-schmandards.com/2005/measuring-text-readability/

6.7 Electronic media

Gone are the days when the only audio-visual aids available to support chalkboards, charts, maps and badly produced printed sheets from either smelly spirit duplicators or black-staining Gestetner printers were slide projectors and 16 mm movie projectors. There were a wide range of slide a sets and film strips the school could buy and many teachers took their own 35 mm coloured slides at their own expense (tax deductable!). Movies could be rented from a state library but they often were old or did not suit the syllabus. There was also the good chance of attaching the reel of film to the projector so that the sprocket teeth shredded the valuable film. When this happened there was much joy amongst the student body. This also happened in the days before long-suffering Teachers Aids were often given such onerous tasks. Students also loved it when the film was reversed.

Overhead Projectors suddenly became the new teaching aid in the classroom and it was used for projecting transparencies made using the new plain-paper photocopier and special transparent sheets but a melted mess if the incorrect transparent film was used. These overhead projectors (OHP) could also be used to project any transparent object and became very useful in showing some chemical reactions, live specimens, and a range of other demonstrations. Coloured clear plastic or cellophane could be used to show colour mixing in art and geographers could draw on transparent map outlines. In the corporate world these were very useful in showing transparencies of financial statements, process flow diagrams or drawing up organisational charts. They are still useful for such purposes today, especially for projecting cartoons onto a chalkboard for tracing.

Move on to the late second half of the 20th Century when black & white, reel-to-reel video recorders were introduced. They also had some threading problems but could be used with school video cameras if one could find a student strong enough to carry the bulky shoulder-carried units.

Gradually computers began to come into schools and other training areas. The early models (e.g. Apple IIE) still had monochrome monitors and large floppy disk drives. If one had some expertise one could write programs to do simple things. I spent several months writing a program in Applesoft Basic which gave revision questions to students with audio feedback if they scored a correct answer. Wow!

In the 2000's, I built a schools intranet system for internal use by all of the school's Faculties. The Principal had come up with the brilliant idea that remote (distance) learning at our second (country) campus would solve the problem of lack of staff at that campus. Unfortunately, setting up the network was an honorary and 'voluntary' position and few of my colleagues wanted to assist expanding their lessons on the framework which I had built. Well, at least my programs became online in the school and then later available through the Internet at home. On this network I had all of my class notes as .pdf files which the students could download at home, multiple slide sets of my photographs, graphic simulations and home-made videos as well as links to more sophisticated pages on the World Wide Web, including practice examinations from the state government. This was great for my classes who had just started to use laptops in class. Some of my colleagues attempted to use this new commercial brand of networked technology but found problems with it. For example, the Head of Languages who knew nothing about computers was 'pressured' into replacing his few PCs by several more 'thin-client' monitor-keyboards which ran off one small section of the school's mainframe. He purchased a very expensive language program which then crashed every time more than six students used it.

Most other teachers who used computers in these early days could handle simple programs such as the common word-processing programs and readers and 'slide' viewers. Some graduated to programs such as Excel and PowerPoint and usually bored their students by their continual use. Computers were mainly limited to teaching Information Technology, but even here, the IT teacher spent most of his time checking for games and Playboy uploads on student monitors. Hacking into the school's mainframe seemed to be a regular event by students who were experts in using (and abusing) the school's computer systems or adding their own gaming programs to it.

I was lucky in that from the year 2000 onwards, I had moved into a new building which, due to an unprecedented decision of the Administration, had been designed partly by the teachers using it. I had an excellent teaching space which had a class set of PCs and a teacher's PC connected to a data projector which gave a good, large image and stereo sound on my large pull-down screen. The students (and staff) were also issued with laptops. The school had also gone over to a commercially-produced system for staff and student access but the early introduction gave many problems because of difficulty in logging in, frequent computer crashes and insufficient speed and memory to handle videos and the like. By then I had further developed my own intranet system which had also been also linked to the school's network and to the Intranet and therefore to the students' homes.

So, you have a laptop or PC and WIFI in your classroom and your students' laptops can upload your material. Good! I hope that you can use it as a main teaching aid to supplement your own teaching rather than replace it. What you have and how you can use electronic media is usually determined by the facilities available at the school or training room. This can vary from none whatsoever to a computer guru's dream of computing facilities with all of the current teaching Apps, social media and other linkages on an international basis. Online video conferencing is great if you can get connected to outlying students, international agencies, companion schools and remote guest speakers.

For those teachers not really comfortable with terms like bios, cache etc. and wish to teach and use some computerised material to add new dimensions to their work, some of the following may be useful:

- store text documents as .pdf files to save memory and reduce unwanted editing using security tabs;

- use any image viewer slideshow function for your own photos or scan/download those appropriate from the internet. Watch for copyright infringements…teachers can get away with a lot, especially if their work is not to be published. American government agencies such as NASA usually allow copyright-free use of their materials and there are some sites on the web especially designed for teachers to use. Some sites (such as technical sites, webcams etc) can also be linked directly via the Internet;

- use JPEG formats rather than the larger memory Bitmap files for images;

- sounds such as foreign phrases, sounds, special talks etc. are best copied as MP3 files. Very useful if they are 'hot-linked' to words or phrases in interactive text documents when teaching languages, cultural studies, music and the like;

- think about storage and ease of access. There is nothing so boring to students than to watch an harassed teacher looking for a lost file in amongst a hard drive filled with thousands of files. Arrange teaching sequences as such in date or use numbered or alphabetically ordered folders on a portable hard drive – say about 1 terabyte;

- use videos as appropriate. Short clips are better than long one. With some skill and a small video camera, one can make videos of places not available to students (mine sites, remote environments, zoos etc.). The best formats are WMV (which play readily on Windows) or MPEG-4 and I have found that the free VLC video player works with most formats but this will have to be downloaded onto student laptops. Video tapes made on excursions are great to review during revision lessons;

- use appropriate and school/institute approved programs and Apps for educational use. There are a wide variety of these but, they must be suitable for the age group of the students and as a good compliment to the lessons. Of course, students will also try to use games and other non-education Apps 'smuggled in' during lessons; watch out for this! Some schools only use approved programs and Apps on their network with the appropriate filter. Any new App must go through the usual approval channels and there are many education Apps which can be used to make student notes, sort out and storing information, teaching English and foreign languages, translators and dictionaries, astronomy and science simulations, art and creative Apps, technical Apps for learning skills and a whole lot more. It takes a search of the Internet and permission to use them as required;

- take care with plagiarism when students complete assignments electronically as there is always the temptation to cut-and-paste large slabs of information from Internet sources and other student's work. Teaching is about creativity and learning within the individual student, not copying large amounts of the work of others. Naturally, some use of accessed information with limited download of written word, images or videos can be allowed but these must have the appropriate acknowledgement just the same as written text has their appropriate references. Some schools and universities have been forced to use anti-plagiarism software such as *Turnitin* and *PapersOwl* to stop cheating but there are some problems with relying on electronic answers to this problem. See:

https://www.affordablecollegesonline.org/college-resource-center/plagiarism-prevention-and-awareness/

https://www.uts.edu.au/current-students/support/helps/self-help-resources/referencing-and-plagiarism/how-avoid-plagiarism

https://www.opencolleges.edu.au/informed/teacher-resources/plagiarism/

https://world.edu/universities-must-stop-relying-on-software-to-deal-with-plagiarism/

- teachers unfortunately need to spend extra time out of their limited spare time in learning how to operate the hardware and use the software effectively. Inservice courses can help, especially if they are given in school time, but some of these are often given by 'experts' who are not teacher/trainers and do not appreciate the time constraints and lack of technical savvy of their audience. I have attended many such courses where the guest speaker is sometimes a 'computer guru' who has difficulty with personal communication in the real world, so one then has to do extra work sorting out how the system actually works;

- teachers also often use their home time and computer programs to make their own electronic resources. For these tasks, they need to have good software (and skills) in:

  - word processing and editing. The free Kindle App allows for viewing of many eBooks on ordinary computers;

  - scanning of documents (perhaps an Optical Character Recognition – OCR – program) and a good scanner;

  - simple video editor and video converter;

  - art/image creation and editing program;

- sound editor and sound file converter;

- HTML or Internet development program if doing one's own web pages;

- decompressing program for compressed files such as WINZIP, WINRAR for opening compressed files or compressing files for email transmission. I use Total Commander for this and a wide range of file-viewing actions; and

- many useful images, videos, sound files, and whole teaching systems are best linked rather than copied. The links (such as those in this book) are easily put into web pages or 'hot linked' into Word documents for ease of use and there are no copyright issues.

There are also many programs available for free download and private use but check with the institution about use in face-to-face teaching. Also, watch out for computer virus and other malware which may come from downloading 'free' material off some dodgy websites. Download some free anti-virus software from only reputable and reliable sites. Do an Internet search to find out about the safety and usefulness of a program proposed for download, and use the word 'forum' in your search to find out what others think about it. Also ask the institution if you may be able to use any of their security software.

Remember that any electronic teaching aid should be:

- supportive of and NOT in place of a lesson;

- appropriate to the lesson prepared;

- of short duration followed by application;

- elicit interest and motivation;

- easily used without the fuss of setting up and workable (especially if using the Internet); and

- reusable for future lessons.

Chapter Seven

Sketching Skills
For
Teachers

7.1 Why sketch?

The ability to sketch, no matter how simple is a very useful tool in teaching and instruction. It does not take much artistic talent to sketch on a chalkboard, whiteboard or computer drawing page and there are many little tricks which the non-artist can use to achieve great results. Some of these tricks, such as tracing from a pencil or faint crayon of a projected cartoon have already been suggested in previous chapters.

The teaching often demands the regular use of diagrams and sketches. These may be:

- formal or

- informal

Formal diagrams are those used to give an accurate representation of some object or principle requiring accuracy of *scale, content* and *colour*. Examples of these would include: scientific sketches e.g. cross-sections of plants, chemical flow charts, physics apparatus; mathematical graphs and charts; technical drawings in engineering; sketches of ancient buildings and dress; geographical representations of surface features and so on.

Such sketches are usually drawn so that students may copy them into their books or upload them to their laptops. Other formal sketches may be simply for elaboration and illustration and may be permanently drawn on paper, a spare chalkboard or saved in an image format.

Whilst many teachers prefer to use copied overhead transparencies or image files, some still wish to do their own unique versions and lead by example when stressing the need for care and artistry in written work.

Informal sketches are often drawn in the midst of normal classroom teaching. If used with flair, they can break up the boredom of "chalk-and-talk" sessions. Moreover, they can be used to:

- motivate the student;

- illustrate abstract ideas;

- aid student memory; and

- put a little joy into learning.

Indeed, some students will remember, with happiness and accuracy a teacher's "weird" sketches used in the classroom.

To give teaching some impact, sketches may be:

- exaggerated e.g. don't draw a "stick-figure" - draw an elephant or some other form;

- made them slightly gross (but *not* too offensive) e.g. don't just draw plants - draw man-eating plants;

- humorous e.g. don't just draw a flow diagram of the natural Water Cycle, draw a diver on a bicycle (then erase and do the real thing!);

- colourful e.g. use many colours in the drawing and encourage students to do the same. Whiteboard sketches can include magnetic "stick-on' sketches prepared in advance;

- topical (without being offensive) e.g. don't draw a picture of a human figure - draw a popular cartoon character such as Homer Simpson;

- consistently "eccentric" - (a little madness helps!) develop a set of simple characters (e.g. Professor Oz used in my classes) to help you teach. These can be taken from or modified from professional well-known cartoons but must be practiced. Copyright should be OK in class but don't publish them.

Make up a story with your characters; and have fun:

Figure 7.1: Professor Oz

BUT REMEMBER - practice makes perfect.

Do not try any "weird" methods unless they have been practiced; your content is correct; your discipline is reasonable (keep control at all times) and you have a very good rapport with your class. Students do not respect fools who talk down to them and draw silly diagrams for their own gratification.

7.2. Basics in using sketching

Once that the need for a drawing has been established, the teacher should clearly define what is to be incorporated into the drawing and what are the objectives to be reached using the drawing.

Part of the careful planning that would go into the successful drawing would include:

• clear knowledge of what is to illustrated

• maturity/ability level of the class

• medium and art material to be used

• intent such as humour; technical description etc.; and

• time and space considerations for the drawing.

Naturally, with experience and long-term knowledge of the class and subject matter, the teacher would be able to make these considerations in a minimum amount of time. Often these considerations are evaluated within the classroom itself.

7.3 Copying sketches and originals

With a little skill and a lot of practice, the teacher may be able to draw simple cartoons and sketches without much difficulty. However, if technical subjects or exact reproductions are to be made then more effort and some innovation is required. These illustrations are best copied from either original illustrations or from well-drawn illustrations made by the teacher when time permitted. Drawings, cartoons and even photographs can be reproduced (as drawings) by means of:

- **plain-paper copiers** for multiple copies, often with the facility of enlargement;

- **computer graphic program and printer** (usually limited to A4 size);

- **grid-square enlargement** in which the original is covered with a transparent grid and the outlines are carefully copied onto a finely-drawn grid of enlarged (or reduced) dimensions. An old-fashioned technique which is still useful. My students, preparing for a school dance, once covered the entire rear wall of an Assembly Hall with a pop artist's face using this technique. Awesome!

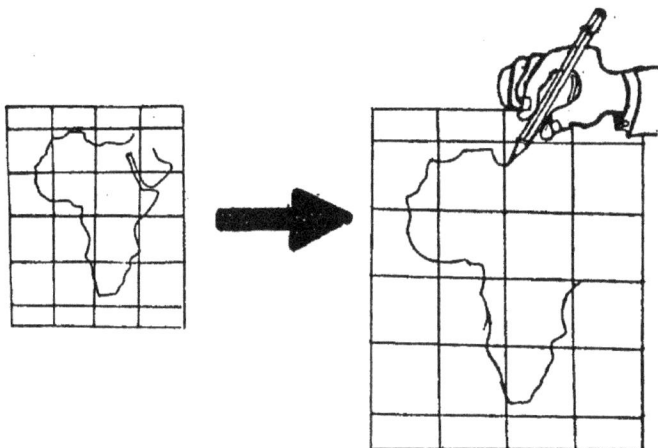

Figure 7.2: Scaling using a grid

- **tracing of the original** using semi-transparent paper. This is only possible if the original is large enough for use in front of the class (so why not use the original?):

- **tracing the original onto a transparency** or sheet of clear plastic using a felt pen. This transparency, no matter how small can then be projected (using a slide projector or an overhead projector) onto a chalkboard or chart-paper for any dimension;

- **small originals can be cut out and projected** if the original is on white paper, very small e.g. (3% mm x 2% mm) and is able to be cut out. The small cutting is then mounted into a cardboard slide mount and made "transparent" by the coating it with a layer of vegetable oil. Some old 'solid projectors' or *epidiascopes'* may be found in some institutions which will project paper photographs, charts etc.

- **large originals can be photographed** and the negative projected to any dimension;

- **use an optical or mechanical drawing aid** such as the draughtsman's *pantograph.*

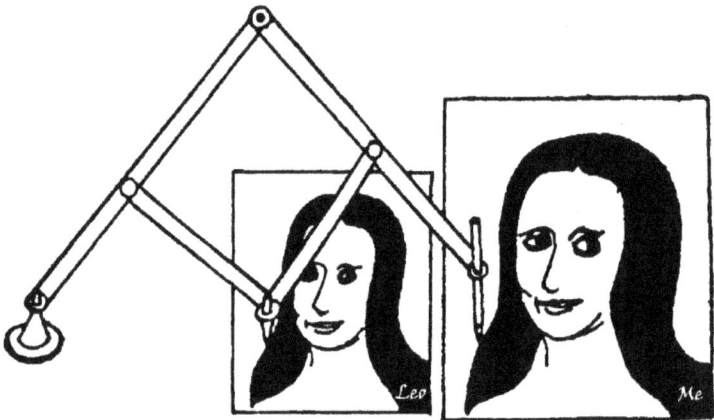

Figure 7.3: Scaling using a pantograph

and

- **using prepared plastic templates (stencils)** of countries, apparatus and other shapes and letters.

By the use of any of the above methods, a teacher without much artistic skill can reproduce almost any drawing or photograph provided that there are no major difficulties with copyright.

7.4 Shapes

Many of the drawings used in education, particularly those drawings constructed in front of the class, are the *sketch* or *cartoon* variety. In order to produce a reasonable drawing other than the "stick figure" type (these can be useful too), the teacher must have some basic ideas of freehand drawing skills. These include the use of shape as most drawings can be constructed of simple geometric shapes.

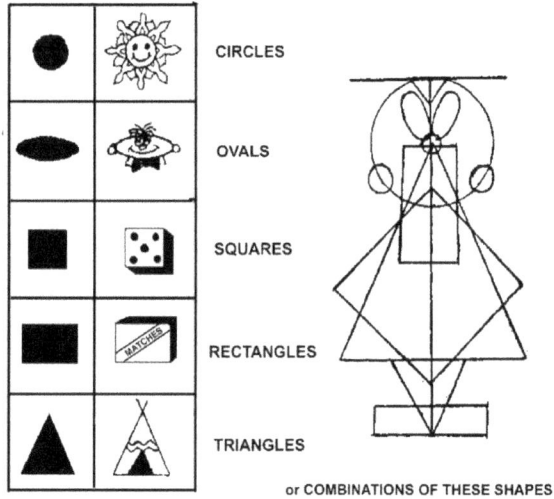

Figure 7.4: Using shapes to start a sketch

Naturally most sketches and drawings are not just simple geometric constructions but these are used as the *framework* around which the drawer can then build the subject of the illustration in freehand using curves, straight lines and shadings:

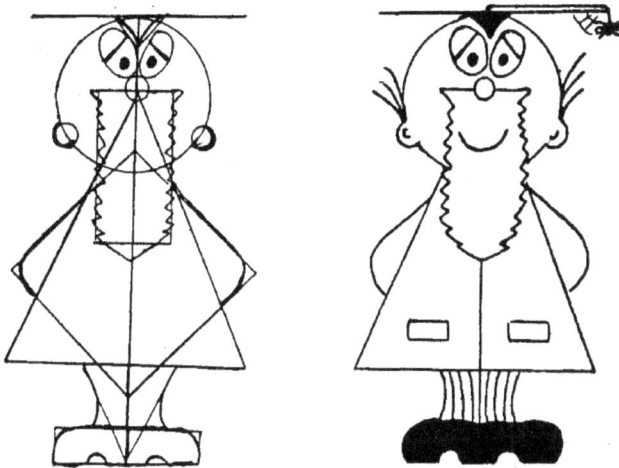

As for inspiration, the best place for this is *real life;* with some exaggeration and distortion to give the drawing some character and humour.

7.5: Lines and angles

Lines may be used for purposes other than connecting and rounding-off geometric patterns to give them a more natural appearance. The type of line can also be used to convey a message about the object or cartoon character. Thin lines infer a delicate, weak object and broad lines suggest strength, smooth lines infer neatness but rough, wrinkled lines suggest untidiness.

Lines can also be used to create an illusion of depth, giving the character some **perspective** with the background. This can be done by drawing more distinct objects much smaller and closer together than objects which are in the foreground:

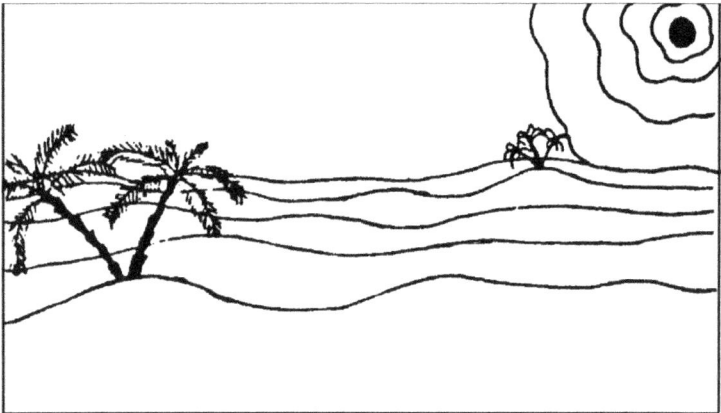

Figure 7.6: Using lines to create distance

Another method which provides perspective is to draw "parallel" lines which recede into the distance and disappear at a point - the **vanishing point**. This is the most common way of giving drawings perspective:

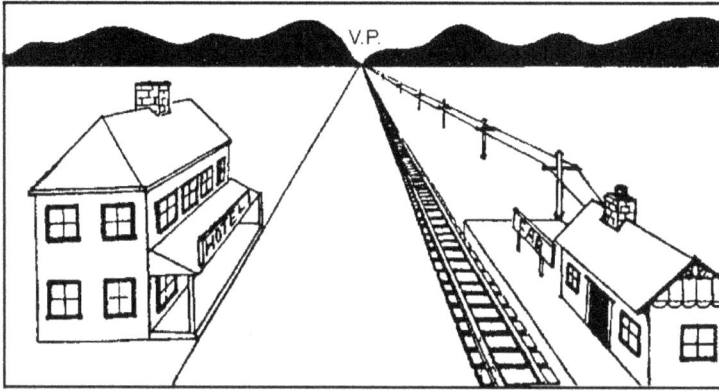

Figure 7.7: The Vanishing Point used for distance

In the above sketch, notice that the illusion of distance is provided by the "horizontal" lines which recede to the vanishing point at the gap in the hills in the background. This also implies that these lines are parallel. The vertical lines (and the horizontal lines in the immediate foreground) are drawn parallel to each other and get smaller in the distance.

Lines going into the distance, such as the top of the roofs of the buildings, the edges of the road and tracks, and the telegraph lines all go to the vanishing point. The artist may use 'construction' lines which are faintly drawn to the vanishing point and then erased later.

The angles which are used to define vanishing points, and there can be more than one vanishing point in the drawing, are important because they establish the position of **eye level** of the observer, the orientation of the sketch and the degree of depth. This is shown in Figure 7.8 below:

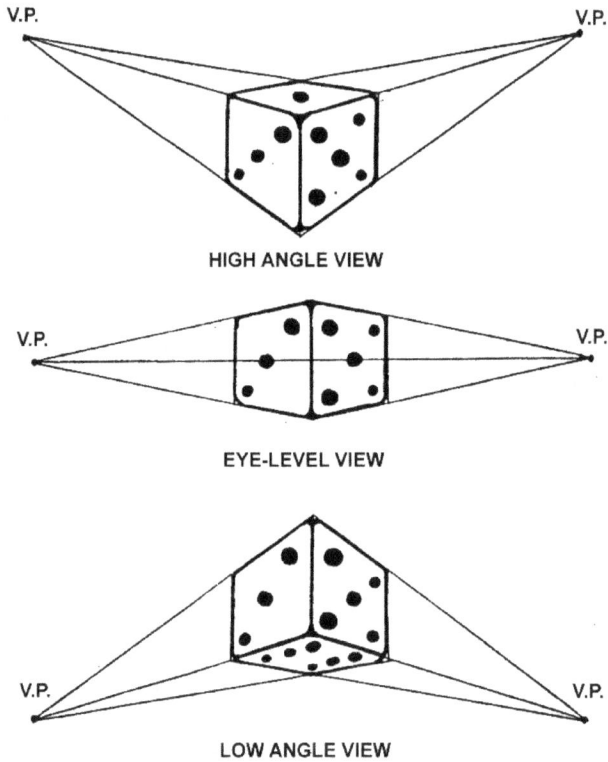

Figure 7.8: The angles of Vanishing Points can give perspective

Distortion can also be achieved by moving the vanishing points away from the same horizontal plane:

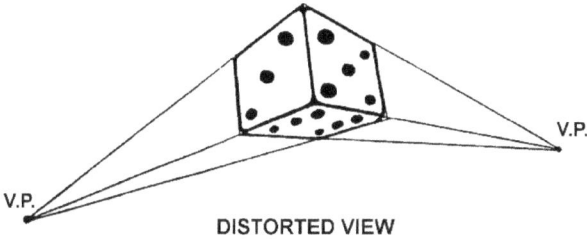

DISTORTED VIEW

Figure 7.9: The Vanishing Point and distortion

7.6 Contrast and shading

Drawings and diagrams are usually constructed so that a class can have their attention focused onto a particular item of educational interest. Often it will be the method used to contrast the object or shade its background that will have the greatest effect in attracting the attention of the class.

Usually in teaching, the best contrast is gained by drawing with a dark pen etc. onto a light background - white is useful such as on a whiteboard, but light yellows, pale pinks, light greens and even light blues can also provide the added interest of colour using a dark pen.

If a chalkboard is used, the colour of the board itself will have an effect on the contrast achieved with different chalks. For good contrast, the following colours are (in order of best contrast):

Black Chalkboard	Green Chalkboard	Blue Chalkboard
Yellow	Yellow	Yellow
White	White	White
Pink	Blue	Pink
Green	Pink	Green
Red	Green	Red
Blue	Red	Blue
Purple	Purple	Purple

In addition, it should be remembered that, at a distance, some outlines are difficult to see so they must be drawn in heavier shades.

Subtle shading of the central object or character will also add to the depth of the drawing. Shadows drawn next to the object can be used to denote time of day or position in relation to a light source:

Figure 7.10: The effect of shading

7.7 Some ideas on lettering

Lettering, other than the normal text of a message, can be used to:

- give the title or heading of information;

- complement a diagram or sketch - captions, action, sounds etc.;

- label parts of a diagram;

- assist with difficult words in spelling training; and

- generally, attract attention.

The incorrect use of lettering can easily spoil an otherwise well-produced drawing or text. The lettering should be appropriate and complement the other visual information. What is to be considered as "appropriate" is largely up to the author of the visual material as long as the combination of the lettering and the rest of the visual image is pleasing to the eye and conveys the intended message.

Some thoughts on the use of lettering may help the reader to develop a sense of **visual harmony**:

Figure 7.11: The use of different lettering

- select a suitable size of lettering that neither distracts from the text or drawing but is not too small to read. In most cases, where the titles and labels support the main work, the lettering could probably be kept to about 1 to 5 times the normal size of the lettering in the text (or of equivalent for drawings);

- upper case titles and labels generally look more pleasing, unless the use of lower-case letters is desired for a special effect, such as in the teaching writing;

- if the lettering is meant to refer to some special event, culture or purpose, then the use of illustrative lettering may be more effective;

- the random mixing of lettering styles, cases and size often distracts from the purpose and is not pleasing to view. Lettering should be consistent;

- different styles of lettering must be used correctly. For example, the seraphs (thin lines at the end of letters) of Roman, Italic and similar styles should not be omitted;

- if the letters are to be read from distances other than normal reading distance (e.g. if on a chalkboard), then they should be drawn thickly and may be bordered with a contrasting shade or colour;

- colour itself can be used for visual effect such as using red for the word 'blood', blue for 'sky' etc.;

- correct spacing is also a lettering technique. Allow a pleasing space between each letter and around the entire lettering. Usually, the mid-lines of each letter (in a vertical plane) are spaced at equal distances;

- sometimes the use of open spaces between words and diagrams is important. A cluttered field of text or drawings is untidy and often difficult to read – typical of the 'fine print' in legal documents;

- if the letters are sloped or are given depth, such features should be retained throughout the same section of letters; and

- lettering should be clean and well organized such as along the same straight line or sloped line. Use faint pencil guidelines (which are later erased) or a graphed backing sheet which can be seen through the paper.

7.8 Some examples

The following examples show some of the motivational sketches which may be used to introduce a topic or simply used as a motivational aid as well as providing some humour to students:

INTRODUCING SCIENCE

Note the use of exaggeration and drama here.

USING CALCULATORS

Old-style version
2 million years BC
(with Memory function)

Note the use of humour here (the 'memory function'
is a knot tied around the five-digit 'calculator')

ART 101

Sometimes the humour is not that subtle. Here, this is obviously a beginner's class.

With a little help from our cultural background (and programs like Photoshop) one can use previous art works but ensure that they are out of copyright or do not contain any offensive material. All sorts of possibilities await you!

(original painting *Landing of Columbus* by John Vanderlyn, 1847)

If you are good at using computer image programs then there are many options open to have a 'straight' but artistic image by varying the contrast/brightness options or using one or several of the 'artistic' processes available on such programs. It looks even better in colour:

Geography

MACHU PICCHU

Happy artistry!

Chapter 8

You be the Judge! – Assessment

8.1 Introduction

Assessment of what has been taught and how it has been taught is the final principle of the three fundamental stages of learning (remember? – 1. Prepare and plan, 2. Maintain and promote the desire to learn and 3. Assess what has been taught). Good teachers are continually assessing their students; albeit most of the time on an informal basis. They may even make simple notations in their Teachers' Diary most lessons but this can be overpowering if overdone.

Any certain stages in the educative process, other stake-holders in the teacher's training may require some feedback as to how each student is performing. The students, their parents and the institution are going to require some sort of feedback on the progress of each student.

This should be:

- based on an unbiased and fair method(s) of assessment. Consideration of cultural and intellectual ability of the class should be considered and hopefully, the teacher should mark all work in an unbiased manner;

- comprehensive so that it covers most of what has been taught. Analysis of the objectives covered and now being tested should always be done;

- valid, in that the assessment instruments actually have assessed what they purport to have tested. This is why all objectives should be clear and well-defined;

- reliable so that they are trustworthy and can be used with similar classes as in formal assessments there is often the need for some comparison between cohorts of students or to some wider benchmark; and

- simple so that all stake-holders understand the outcome of the assessment and can see the strengths and weakness of the individual student.

This latter point is often overlooked by educators who are intently involved in assessment on a wider scale. Regular assessment, usually on an informal basis, is done by the classroom teacher/instructor for the purpose of seeing how individual students are learning as they are being taught. This is done to find both the strengths and weakness of each student at every stage of the teaching process. Of course, it is difficult to assess every student during a lesson so any informal assessment may be spread over several 'revision' lessons and there may be a need for some more formal assessment at the end of each topic or skill training.

8.2 Assessment methods

As mentioned, these can be applied either informally during class time or formally at some pre-arranged time (well-in advance to give students warning). Each may include:

- simple questions either verbally in class or as written tests;

- demonstrations by individuals or group of some physical skill such as a sporting, gymnastic, artistic or drill movement or performance;

- a competitive debate, discussion, short music, video, recitation or mime production;

- samples of creative writing such as poems, short plays or stories;

- a rating scale of the Likert variety of 1 to 5; or

- observation of personal or group dynamics or performance in various situations.

There are many ways of assessment, including self-appraisal such as a reflection about one's own performance with some diary or checklist notation. New teachers may even like to do this by making a video recording of their teaching style (with class approval). Doing this, one soon becomes aware of those little eccentricities of speech, mannerism and appearance which students love to copy or exaggerate. Ummmm! Like! You know! Yeah! What's that?

8.3 Who does the assessment?

Formally, the teacher/instructor may not have much of a choice when it comes to major periods of assessment as these may be planned and provided by some external authority, such as a State education system or the institution. Assessment on a formal basis may be 'School-based' or 'Externally-based'. I have been lucky (??) in having taught in both systems and was an examiner or appraiser of school assessments in both types of systems at the State level. There has been considerable argument about the benefits or failures of each system.

In a **'school-based system'**, assessment items are designed and administered by the teachers within the school continually over a set time-period, say the two final years of Secondary schooling. Samples of this assessment, probably consisting of all of the formal assessment items (and required answers) as well as samples of the actual students' work at each award grade were then sent in at set times to some central reviewing panel. These were then evaluated externally by a review panel charged with assessing standards, making comparisons with other schools and possibly approving (or not) the final grades which were to be allocated to all of the students in that cohort.

Teachers are usually given considerable guidance in how to set their own assessment items and how to prepare submissions for the government review sessions. Having been on a State Review Panel for secondary schools for over twenty years as well as being the Head of a syllabus committee which set down what and how my subject was to be taught and assessed, I found that such a school-based system usually gave a fair estimation of the worth of the students in that subject.

The members of my review panel were all experienced teachers who (mostly) also had to design and administer their students' assessment items. They also had to prepare their own submissions for review by the panel (but NOT by themselves!) and so knew about appropriate and acceptable standards as well as all of the 'tricks-of-the-trade' which teachers might use to bolster student grades or generally fudge results.

Teachers who were lacking expertise in this subject were often invited to join the review panel on a temporary basis to see how the system worked and to be given advice. Usually these were the unfortunate teachers who had been 'volunteered' by their Head of Department to teach a subject for which they were not qualified to teach. Schools were also visited as requested by members of the review panel to assist such teachers should there be a perceived need.

Whilst such a system generally worked well, it was not an easy one to operate and there was often pressure from those who would then take on these assessed students; namely universities, colleges and employer groups. There was also considerable debate about categories of objectives and which assessment items were formative or summative.

Formative assessments are those assessment items which evaluate how someone is learning throughout the course in the classroom. These could be simple written tests, skills tests, quizzes, games, projects, presentations and group activities. **Summative assessments** are evaluations of what someone has learned throughout a course.

Formative assessment could include such items as questions at the end of the lesson, simple written tests, individual skills tests, quizzes, games, projects, field reports, presentations and group activities. They would occur as a natural part of the teacher's preparation, planning and lesson presentation. Grading and feedback would then be given to students and parents so that any remedial action could be instantly given.

Summative assessments often take place at the end of a course, specific unit of work or as formal mid-year/year or semester examinations. They could also include major items performed throughout the year such as specific projects or skills/practical reports.

In a school-based system, summative assessment grades could also be cumulative, that is they would collectively add to the final assessment of the student at the end of the program or period of schooling. There may be some 'weighting' applied to those items given at various periods throughout the total program e.g. assessment items (such as a mid-semester exam) at the beginning of the program would be weighted less than a similar assessment item at the end of the program. They could then be used to derive a final grade for some exiting the system.

Problems with school-based assessment included:

- expertise needed by teachers to set and grade valid and reliable test instruments, especially in discerning what would be formative and what would be summative;

- some assessments such as essays and projects could involve plagiarism and copying of other student's work;

- considerable time required by teachers to collate and prepare individual student portfolios of summative work;

- some difficult internal comparison of the grades of students and the respective overall merits of these portfolios had to be made so that a representative selection could be sent in for review. This was a major activity in schools and many education systems would close their schools down for several 'student-free' days for this purpose; a major problem for parents;

- time off for those teachers on the review panels of was required for several days at various times of the year to carry out review. This often required the use of relief teachers to take their place and the usual extra preparation by those being relieved to do review panel work;

• during review there would be considerable comparison of the school portfolios with each school being reviewed several times. This was often a difficult task for those doing the review as schools sometimes varied greatly in standards of the students' work;

• some schools would also use either simplistic or over-complicated methods of assessment which made comparisons difficult. For example, one school had a Head of Department who saw statistical analysis as the main way to compare their student's work and would 'scale -up' their uniformly poor performances using some advanced statistics. They argued that this was necessary as their assessment instruments were always of an extremely high standard. In return, it was argued that such statistics inflated measurement of student performance and that the assessment instruments should have been set at an appropriate level in the first place. Other schools, especially with unqualified teachers, set assessment instruments well below the standards required by the syllabus and had to be given some support; and

- there was also some suspicion by future stakeholders such as universities, that students were not assessed adequately by such a system; especially by those institutions who had long since used the more traditional approach of formal examinations or in-house performance assessment. Moreover, parents of students assessed in this manner did not understand the system and also had doubts about its validity.

In an **'externally-based' system** the summative assessment of the student would be set by some external authority and distributed formally and at set times to schools. This is the old traditional system of formal examination which is still in operation in many countries. These formal examinations could be also be sat and supervised externally and then graded by (hopefully) professional examiners who would then release the individual student grades back to the schools. In my early days as a teacher, I had been appointed as a paid 'Examiner' and had spent many hours at night over more than a week in a cold public building, along with hundreds of other 'Examiners' in all subjects, marking a section of the 'Yearly Exam' in my subject. Most of my fellow examiners were also fellow teachers who knew their subject, but a minority had been given the job because of 'contacts' in the government or elsewhere and were not as well qualified but at least had some paid work.

Criticism of externally-based assessment had often led to the development of school-based assessment systems on the premise that schools knew their own students better than external examiners. Some of the criticism for externally-based summative assessment included:

- students had to remember an enormous amount of content over a lengthy period of time;

- assessment by this method was very content oriented and did not measure any of the practical skills and sometimes true understanding of what was taught in the classroom over a long time;

- 'cramming' for exams became a major activity both in the school and at home and there was a well-established 'industry' of literature, personal tutors and 'coaching colleges' for this purpose. Whilst revision is a necessary part of learning, the final term of many institutions sometimes was devoted to nothing but preparation for such examinations. It was a problem with some essay-based exams such as in History or the Social Sciences that students (and teachers) would often cram for 'expected' questions which regularly featured in the major exam. Woe betide any student who crammed the wrong topics;

- cramming also lead to the use of 'memory aids' by which whole slabs of the content could be learnt off by memory rather than knowing what such content really meant and what it was useful for in real life. This crammed content was then quickly forgotten after the exam as the student did not see its relevance, application nor really understand it in the first place;

- examinations were often administered under strict formal conditions which often gave students massive anxiety and other psychological problems both before, during and after the examination;

- en-mass examinations in large halls which are difficult to supervise could encourage cheating such as hidden notes and the use of equally hidden mobile (cell) phones with earplugs;

- marking of these summative assessments were also subject to questions about standards used, especially if the whole instrument was marked by one person only and not subject to multiple assessment. Such complaints may or may not have been justified as the students may not have had any idea of the criteria used in the assessment;

- written examinations used solely for any final summative assessment often tested other things as well as the objectives used in teaching. Language expression, cultural differences, deficiencies in mathematics, learning and emotional differences and recent personal problems were just a few of the 'incidental' factors which affected the student's response to the external exam.

With arguments for and against both systems of assessment, it seemed logical that a combination of both could be a better alternative to a method which used only a school-based assessment or an externally-based examination. Some education authorities suggest that a school-based approach could be used but moderated for comparisons to standards and between schools using an externally-set final exam. This might alleviate some of the problems but maintain others.

Education authorities seem to vary in their approach depending upon the political climate at the time. In many cases, an authority may have a system which is driven by university or college entrance criteria using a final examination, sometimes with a combination of school-based assessment.

Students at the end of their Secondary education will naturally become very intense about such a system and will strive for the best score(s) possible even if they have little idea as to what they will do with it in the following year. There is also the worrying period between doing the external exams and then waiting until they are processed and the grades or evaluation is sent out.

Also, some more enlightened universities often prefer other entrance 'qualifications' such as a Curriculum Vitae (CV or personal account of one's experience) and an interview with previous work experience also being considered.

The final vague statistical assessment result often required additional support for those students who did not wish to enter a university but follow another, equally important career pathway. Moreover, whilst attendance at Secondary School until the final year is usually considered the norm, many students may wish to leave early and gain apprenticeships or cadetships in various non-university placements.

The final pre-university assessment system may be quite complicated and often beyond the comprehension of parents (and many students and educators as well!). For example, the ATAR (Australian Tertiary Admissions Rank) system attempts to provide a common statistical score based on several criteria involving all students. An explanation of this can be found at:

https://www.tutoringforexcellence.com.au/blog/wh at-is-an-atar-a-simple-explanation-for-parents-students-and-teachers/

https://www.uac.edu.au/media-releases/fact-sheet-all-about-the-atar

Whatever the assessment system, the classroom teacher is often the best judge of a student's performance and should be given opportunities to express this performance to parents and future institutions and employers. Often this may be a personal assessment given as a personal reference and so it is up to the individual teacher to be very good at accurately assessing the total worth of each of their students.

Some useful articles on formative and summative assessment can be found at:

https://www.oecd.org/site/educeri21st/40600533.pdf

https://www.education.act.gov.au/__data/assets/pdf_file /0011/297182/Teachers-Guide-To-Assessment.pdf

8.4 Written assessment items

In many teaching situations, written tests, examinations and surveys are perhaps the most common. These can vary from simple in-class tests of a formative nature to a final Term Examination given over an extended period of time in a formal setting. In class, a simple written test may be used to quickly find out what students have remembered. It may take the form of a few simple questions, a dictation for the spelling of words, a list for the recall of facts, a simple set of maths problems or even may be a simple game in which students are given a time limit to recall facts or a team quiz.

The secret of constructing good assessment instruments, whether they be in written or physical response format, is to have clear and well-constructed lesson objectives in the first place.

Written assessment items could be of several forms:

- multi-choice;

- single response;

- extended response; or

- essay type items.

Multi-choice items pose a question in simple terms and a choice of four (usually) or five answers are provided; the student having to select only one of these. These can be constructed from a variety of objectives and use a variety of question stimuli such as a simple written question, a series of diagrams, photographs, a mathematical problem, or if the test is given electronically, a video clip, animation or sound file.

Good four-response multichoice questions will consist of a simple stem or question given so that only <u>one</u> response is needed. Multi-barrelled questions are confusing unless there is a connection e.g.

"who is credited with discovering America and in what year? – "

The choice of answers should contain:

- an answer that is correct all of the time e.g.

(a) Christopher Columbus in 1492;

- a 'distractor' , a wrong answer which may be considered correct by students who do not know their work as well as they should e.g.
  (b) The Pilgrim Fathers in 1620;

- and two totally wrong answers e.g.
  (c) Amerigo Vespucci, 1501;
  (d) George Washington 1770.

If the teacher has good rapport with the class and this test is formative, he/she may even put in an <u>occasional</u> funny answer to relieve the tension e.g.

(d) Kinney Records (UK) 1971
(this was the rock band 'America')

'Mix and Match' could be considered as another version of 'multi-choice' as it too gives the answers and could receive an unintelligent correct answer by guesswork. In this type of item, several questions and answers are given and the student is asked to match each question with the appropriate answer e.g.

(1) who is credited with the discovery of America;

(2) reached Brazil in 1501;

(3) Is considered the 'Founding Father' of America

(4) Amongst the first settlers of America.

Choices:

(a) George Washington;

(b) The Pilgrim Fathers;

(c) Christopher Columbus;

(d) Amerigo Vespucci.

They are scored by the number of correct responses e.g. if the student gave the following responses:

1c; 2a; 3d and 4b, then they would receive a score for 2 correct.

Sometimes, teachers may give fractions of a point for simple answers, especially large banks of multichoice items (not a good idea!), assigning say, ½ mark or even more absurd fractions. This only causes headaches in marking and tallying and I much prefer giving a simple one mark for each simple item.

Single response questions are also given to test simple recall. They can be very simple such as a requiring a name, date or mathematical answer such as (<u>answers</u> given here in case you don't know!):

1. Who is credited with the discovery of America? <u>Christopher Columbus</u> (1 mark)
   or
1. In which year did Amerigo Vespucci reach Brazil? <u>1501</u> (I mark)
   or
1. Calculate 3 + 6 x (5 + 4) ÷ 3 – 7 <u>14</u> (1 mark)
   (remember: Please Excuse My Dear Aunt Sally)

Usually, such items are given as a bank of questions as part of an overall larger test instrument. Instruments consisting wholly of multi-choice or short single response are limited in testing only recall or simple language or mathematical skills – and are quite boring to the student leading to 'exam fatigue' in which the student 'switches off' in clear thinking and starts to make guesses such as falling for the 'distractor' as it seems obvious or selecting the same letter for every multi-choice question.

Such questions are easy to mark, especially if the test instrument is set out so that the appropriate response (as a letter or number) is placed down the edge of the test paper allowing for quick eye response or even some answer template that is placed over the responses. In some electronic systems, these can also be marked by optical methods if the responses are made on a card requiring the answers to be shaded in sections of the 'answer sheet'.

Extended response questions can allow for a great deal of variation by the teacher in testing the pre-arranged unit objectives, especially those of the so-called 'higher order' knowledge objectives and also some non-manipulative skills such as those encountered in mathematics, sciences and languages. They will use verbs to request the student to not only actively recall knowledge, but to use it to show their worth in such more thoughtful processes of comprehension, application, analysis, synthesis, evaluation, organizing, calculation and classifying etc.

Some examples could include:

1) In a geological laboratory four minerals have been mislabelled. They are all white and have been powdered. The minerals are:
BARYTE, CALCITE, QUARTZ and SMITHSONITE (Zinc Carbonate).

Design a set of **chemical tests** which could be used to prove which white powder was which mineral. Give the full **method and the results** which should occur for each test. (You may use a list or flow diagram with notes.)

(your go!)

(2 to 4 marks depending upon the criteria require such as choice of tests; sequence of testing; accuracy of results of tests; structure of setting out)

2) Compare and contrast the attitudes of Caesar and Pompey towards their defeated enemies.

(2 to 4 marks depending upon genuine comparisons/contrasts given and their number)

These questions can be more of a challenge as they usually require the application of knowledge in a variety of ways. Teachers should be aware of this and balance these questions out with some of the simpler recall types.

Essay type items are a further extension of extended items because they require a degree of organisation, logical sequencing and comprehension as well as the knowledge required to answer the question.

Students are usually practiced at doing such questions through the use of formative essays as assignments or in-class activities. Students with language difficulties and who have little concept of structure and sequencing will have problems with such questions, even if they have a great knowledge of the subject matter.

In essays and assignments, students are obliged to do their own work and acknowledge the contribution, quotations and data and other uses of external sources. In universities, especially at the Post-graduate level, referencing can be very proscriptive. The Harvard (sometimes known as the 'Author Date' system), Chicago citation and American Psychological Association (APA) methods seem to be the most practical reference systems. Some useful links to guides on referencing are at:

https://library.lit.ie/wp-content/uploads/2017/10/WriteitRightPDFOct2017.pdf (Harvard)

https://library.westernsydney.edu.au/main/sites/default/files/pdf/cite_Harvard.pdf (Harvard)

https://library.westernsydney.edu.au/main/sites/default/files/cite_Chicago.pdf (Chicago)

https://library.westernsydney.edu.au/main/sites/default/files/pdf/cite_APA.pdf (APA)

https://www.waikato.ac.nz/__data/assets/pdf_file/0014/236120/apa-quick-guide.pdf (APA) https://utslib-drupal-library.storage.googleapis.com/public/attachments/page/apareferencingguide.pdf (APA)

There is always the problem of recurring themes and student anticipation. I remember in my own education, when history exams consisted of a final 3-hour exam at the end of the Senior Year always seem to have questions about:

a. The rise of Germany in the 19th century;
b. Italian nationalism;
c. The emergence of Japan as a modern state; and
d. The causes of the First World War.

In such an exam, students were often asked to select four (out of about six choices) and write an extended essay on the subject (usually of 4+ pages). Students who then prepared six or so essays (often learnt off by heart) and found that their choices did not appear were in real trouble due to their limited knowledge on the other topics.

Essay questions are good at testing the communication skills of the students. They must know the language and be able to use good expression, sequencing, spelling etc. as well as having some knowledge of the subject matter. These questions are good for older Secondary students and adults but they must be aware of the standards required in their use of expression.

A good guide for writing and grading essays can be found at:
http://www.docs.hss.ed.ac.uk/iad/Learning_teaching/Tutors/Handbook/Tutors-Chapter6.pdf

Often, essays and some extended answer questions are graded using a 'rubric' or grid showing the various criteria which is assessed and the levels in each to score a certain grade. An example of this is shown at:

http://home.snu.edu/~hculbert/criteria.pdf and

https://lsa.umich.edu/content/dam/sweetland-assets/sweetland-documents/teachingresources/GivingFeedbackonStudentWriting/Sample_EssayGradingRubric.pdf

8.5 Using rubrics to assess essays and performances

Rubrics, or tables of assessment criteria, are useful for assessments requiring several levels for each of several criteria. They can be set up using the appropriate objectives (the criteria) and the degree to which these will have to be achieved to get a specific grade. They can also be constructed for the assessment of manipulative skills.

Often, they will have the criteria which is to be assessed as a vertical column and the degrees or levels of the performance of each criterion (and their grades) along the horizontal axis of the rubric grid. These can be used in their 'raw state' as a diagnostic 'chart' or even a performance assessment using some sort of aggregate system where the levels of the criteria are assigned grades or even numbers which can then be averaged to obtain a single outcome (rather dubious!). For example, there used to be a <u>fictional</u> and <u>humorous</u> rubric for evaluating military rank and whilst this would be an unfortunate system to use, it does illustrate how a rubric is constructed and how it might be used (or abused) in military assessment. It is an abbreviated version of a common view of the capabilities of Army rank often circulated by juvenile cadets within Officer Training Units. Consider the following assessment scores (shaded):

Criteria	Expectations (Army Company Ranks)			
Score /4	4	3	2	1
Climbing and jumping	Lifts buildings and walks underneath	Leaps small buildings with a run up	Runs into buildings	Falls over doorsteps
Power rating	Kicks locos off tracks	Almost as strong as a loco	Recognises a loco 2 out of 3 times	Says "look at the choo-choo"
Speed	Catches speeding bullets in teeth	Faster than a pistol bullet	Is not issued ammunition	Wets himself with a water pistol
Spiritual ability	He IS god!	Talks to god with permission	Talks to the OC's portrait	Mumbles to himself

Figure 8.1 A fantasy rubric for Army performance

The candidate now could be given a verbal (or printed copy) assessment using the descriptors of the rubric or may be given an 'overall score' or 'grade average' based on the summation or averaging of the numerical values assigned to each level and graded against set standards e.g.

Major (Officer Commanding a Company)   4.00
Captain   3.00
First Lieutenant   2.00
Second Lieutenant   1.00

in this example, the <u>average value</u> of the candidate's assessment (in Figure 8.1) would be (2 + 1 + 3 + 1) /4 or 1.75 – almost attaining the rank of First Lieutenant, an encouraging sign for a Second Lieutenant in training but a disaster for one currently holding that rank.

Rubrics can be **holistic** or **analytic** and be graded using alphabetical or numerical depending upon the needs of the institution doing the assessment. It is very important that the student and any other stakeholder (such as parents) fully understand the nature of the rubric and what it means overall.

Holistic rubrics may offer performance descriptors for each of several levels such as (for four levels):

Needs Improvement,
Satisfactory,
Good,
Accomplished

Some further information on using rubric assessment can be found at:

https://elearning.qmul.ac.uk/guide/marking-an-assignment-using-a-rubric/

https://teaching.uwo.ca/teaching/assessing/grading-rubrics.html

https://teaching.unsw.edu.au/assessment-rubrics

Some more useful blank forms for the DIY development of skills rubrics can be found at:

https://www.gov.nl.ca/education/files/k12_curriculum_guides_kcurriculum_appendix_d_july_28.pdf

A good general guide for teaching motor skills with a guide on using rubrics is given at:

https://www.education.vic.gov.au/Documents/school/teachers/teachingresources/social/physed/fmsteacher.pdf

Teaching and assessing in the Performing Arts is also discussed at:
https://maeia-artsednetwork.org/wp-content/uploads/2016/12/ASD-Combined-Sept2016-cp-er-cp_REV.pdf

8.6 Grading debates and public speaking

Grading a debate in which the students must show some competitive skills in public speaking often goes more into the emotional side of the speakers as well as their performance. Criteria here can be more subjective and may depend also on the degree of difficulty of the subject matter. Some examples of such rubrics are given at:

https://fye.uconn.edu/wp-content/uploads/sites/435/2020/02/Debate-Rubric.pdf

and

http://mahabalipuram-
history.yolasite.com/resources/classroom_debate_r
ubric.pdf

8.7 Assessing attitudes and opinions

Attitude Objectives can be assessed subjectively by
teacher-observation and conversation, but this form
of open assessment can be vague and contain bias.
Moreover, if it is to be done over an extended period
(ideal), then it requires a rather complex system of
recording. Some diligent teachers often attempt to
make daily positive/negative notations about
behaviour and student opinion in their diaries but
this becomes a major and often odious task which
interferes with the teaching process.

Another way of assessing attitudes or opinions with
less subjectivity is by using a Likert-Scale grade of 1
(lowest rating) to 5 (highest rating):

https://www.edu.gov.mb.ca/k12/cur/socstud/frame
_found_sr2/g_blms/g-15.pdf

If a test instrument is written or given as a verbal test
(with or without visual or sound cues), then such

ratings can be totalled and averaged as a numerical score. One must remember, however that the student may not be honest in such tests and give an 'expected' answer or may anticipate the giving of sound cues. Setting the stimulus for written attitude tests can be very difficult if one expects an honest answer.

For example, if the student is shown a photograph of a smog-ridden city with chimney stacks belching smoke and given a 1 to 5 scale of 'liveability', it might be expected that an expected bias would be shown. Given a scale of 1 (almost unliveable) to 5 (a great place to live) a student may feel that they have to prove an 'appropriate green' attitude by selecting an answer of 5. Not a great question because another student coming from such a place and valuing industrialisation could be just as correct in choosing an answer of 1!

Still, Likert rating scales are useful when given as answer choices to general, open-ended questions, especially when determining attitudes or opinions about things or even oneself.

8.8 The use and abuse of statistics

As a schoolboy, I was subject to internal examinations twice a year which were marked as percentages and 50% was considered a pass mark. 49 ½ % was a failure and if it occurred in too many subjects resulted in the poor unfortunate having to stay back and repeat the year. As a 17-year-old trainee teacher, I remember teaching students during my first Practice Teaching session who were older than I because they had failed several years and had to repeat a year or two. The smarter students in this category soon got the message and left school at 15 (then the minimum age) and got a job, an apprenticeship or a place in a secretarial college.

There were external examinations then, set by the State Education Department under great security and given at an exact 'exam period' at the end of Third Form as an Intermediate Examination (for 15-year olds) and at the end of Fifth Form as a Leaving Certificate (for 17-year olds). They were marked externally and grades were given as an alphabetical score, A to E with A, B and C considered as 'passes'. One had to get a good set of grades (?) to matriculate to university and of course, be able to pay the high fees. In the 1960's only about 2% did this and then many of these had been able to get scholarships to pay for the fees.

Gradually some schools saw that teachers and their test instruments were subject to variation – some teachers were considered 'easy markers' and some 'hard'. Eventually, internal assessments were also given to reflect what was being done elsewhere and so students were often awarded grades either in an alphabetical grading, sometimes with + or – internal divisions. A grade of C- was considered a 'borderline' pass and the student was advised to work harder.

Some schools followed government directives or trends and award grades in terms of simple descriptors and there were often conversion grids to convert the raw percentages from test instruments to these descriptors e.g.

GRADE	MARKS RANGE
Very High Achievement	80-100
High Achievement	65-79%
Sound Achievement	45-64%
Limited Achievement	25-44%
Very Limited Achievement	0-24%

Figure 8.2: An achievement score grid

These often still relied on the use of 'cut-off' and it was not uncommon for a teacher to remark certain instruments so that a student should just 'scrape over' into a higher level. Internally this made use of the teacher's intimate knowledge of the student who was seen as having 'good' or 'bad' luck with certain instruments or had natural ability but was deficient in exam technique, mathematics or language.

I remember being in one traditional but dysfunctional school where I was given a class of 'slow learners' to teach. This class was in Grade 7, the lowest year in Secondary school but contained students from ages 11 to 14, many of who had repeated the year and some several times because they could not pass the internal yearly exam. Most couldn't speak English and some were truly intellectually handicapped. I was considered qualified to teach these poor students (some of whom already had Police records!) because I was the youngest teacher in the school in my subject area and did not yet have a university degree. The other teachers of this class had similar qualifications. Students who showed some promise (as their English comprehension improved) were promoted out into mainstream classes where they eventually did well. To do this, my colleagues and I usually collaboratively 're-marked' their papers and then requested their 'promotions' to other classes. The other students were helped as best we could and often plotted with the school's Career Advisor to get them a job after they left at 15 without any suitable school qualifications. Dreadful!

Soon, and in a school-based assessment system, assessment had become very complicated and summative assessment using rubrics, conversions and descriptors became the norm for individual test instruments such as assignments, essays and the like which were then tallied by addition or 'eye-balling' from a grid of such grades for the final evaluation of the student.

For example, the rubric for an assignment on a case study of an Earth hazard (earthquakes, volcanoes etc.) could be structured as that shown on the next page. Notice that as well as descriptors for each level, alphabetical and numerical grades are given for later tallying for some composite grade:

OBJECTIVES	A	B	C	D	E
To recall Knowledge	Very comprehensive and accurate collection of recalled facts about the hazard	Good selection of accurate facts concerning this hazard outlined with some detail	recalls basic knowledge in most areas about this hazard	recalls some knowledge in several areas	recalls some knowledge
To understand concepts	demonstrates a clear understanding of concepts in depth in most areas	demonstrates a clear understanding of concepts in most areas	demonstrates a broad understanding of concepts in most areas with few misconceptions	demonstrates some understanding of concepts in several areas but with many misconceptions	demonstrates some understanding of a few concepts
To apply knowledge & understanding	evaluates both the relevance and scientific merit of information provided in or derived from earth science contexts	evaluates the relevance of information provided in or derived from earth science contexts	selects some relevant information from that provided in or derived from earth science contexts	uses information but does not reflect on its relevance and/or scientific merit	uses some information
Grade	A+ A A-	B+ B B-	C+ C C-	D+ D D-	E+ E E-
Mark	5.0 4.5 4.0	4.0 3.5 3.5	3.0 2.5 2.5	2.0 1.5 1.5	1.0 1.0 0.5

Figure 8.3 A typical rubric for an assignment

Once the various grades for each summative assessment instrument had been tallied (using numerical scores) for each objective category, then the totals could be plotted on a chart to get the overall assessment level.

In the example given on the next page, the Objective Categories are Knowledge, Working Scientifically and Using Information Scientifically (greatly varied from Bloom's Taxonomy) and each Level of Attainment (from Very Low Achievement to Very High Achievement) has been subdivided into ten levels. Student totals are then plotted for each Objective Category and then 'eye-balled' (a dubious technique) by estimating the final overall position by judging the relative spacing between each Objective Category score. In this example, the student would be given an overall achievement in this subject as a High Achievement Grade 7 (HA 7).

Exit Level Grid

K KNOWLEDGE CONC. UND. & APP.	W WORKING SCIENTIFICALLY	U USING INFO. SCIENTIFICALLY	OVERALL LEVEL	LEVEL
				VHA 10
				VHA 9
90				VHA 8
				VHA 7
				VHA 6
				VHA 5
85				VHA 4
				VHA 3
				VHA 2
80				VHA 1
	★			HA 10
				HA 9
75				HA 8
★		★		HA 7
				HA 6
				HA 5
70		★		HA 4
				HA 3
				HA 2
65				HA 1
				8A 10
				8A 9
				8A 8
58				8A 7
				8A 6
				8A 5
52				8A 4
				8A 3
				8A 2
45				8A 1
				LA 10
				LA 9
				LA 8
38				LA 7
				LA 6
				LA 5
32				LA 4
				LA 3
				LA 2
25				LA 1
				VLA 10
				VLA 9
				VLA 8
20				VLA 7
				VLA 6
				VLA 5
15				VLA 4
				VLA 3
				VLA 2
				VLA 1

Figure 8.4 An Exit Grid for achievement

"Lies, damned lies, and statistics" is a phrase erroneously attributed to the author Mark Twain who used this phrase, but erroneously attributed it to the British Prime Minister Benjamin Disraeli. This phrase generally described problems encountered with statistics and how they could be used in many ways as persuasive power. We see the abuse of statistics each day in the media who love to quote numbers or percentages about the success of one commercial product over others or (even worse) political polls forecasting the outcome of an election.

Schools are also lumped into this media fixation with real or imaginary numbers (my apologies to real mathematicians!) as a result of their relative performance in public examinations.

Students and parents usually regard statistics at a very simple level. Usually, most students and parents will understand simple percentages, alphabetical or even descriptor grades. Some might wish to query how the grade was given and this is where teachers must be prepared to put some effort and fairness into their assessment because they are answerable ultimately to the parents of students as well as to the educational authority. Adult students also are usually more discerning and seek to know how they were assessed. This is why assessment MUST be understandable, if not simple, and must be given in terms that all stakeholders can understand.

Many statistical analyses done within schools and other educational institutions usually follow the usual practice of using population statistics. Of these, the **mean** (or average given as x-bar $\bar{x}$) is well understood by most people. This is the value found by adding up all of the scores (e.g. a student's marks over several exams) and dividing it by the number of items:

$$\textbf{mean} = \frac{\text{score } 1 + \text{score } 2 \dots \text{score } n}{\text{number of scores (n)}}$$

or in mathematical terms:

$$\bar{x} = \frac{x_1 + x_2 + x_3 \dots x_n}{n}$$

This assumes that the weighting for each test is the same and that maximum value for the test items is the same. For example, if all tests are of equal value and are given in percentages, then an average of the percentages is probably valid.

This average score for the student may be compared to that of the entire class or bigger cohort also as a class average of all of other student's averages. It may also be compared to a middle score or **median** such as the classic 50% grade.

Parents often wish to know how their student performed in comparison to others in the cohort. This is where letter grades or descriptors such as Very High Achievement are more understandable because they do give some comparison.

Percentages are often deceptive. I remember having an exchange student from another country where, for reasons of esteem, percentages were often inflated. He was used to getting an 80% grade which was in the middle range of his fellow students. In my glass, getting a good grade of 70% in an advanced physics exam was (for him) a disaster and he fretted about telling his parents of his 'failure'.

Some statistically-savvy teachers may dabble in the complexity of higher statistics such as using standard deviations to express some idea of how far away a student might be from the class average. In simple terms, the **Standard Deviation (SD or sigma**

σ) is a measure of the amount of variation from the average (mean) of a set of scores in a population. It is a measure of the spread of the results in a set of scores. A low standard deviation suggests that the student scores tend to be close to the mean, while a high standard deviation indicates that the scores are spread out over a wider range. Standard Deviation is an average of the differences between the scores and the mean of that population. Usually, to get over any negative values in some statistics, the following calculations are made to find the SD:

1. work out the Mean (the simple average of the numbers);
2. subtract the Mean from each score (this is where a negative may occur);
3. square the result;
4. find the mean of those squared differences;
5. take the square root of that mean to get the SD.

In mathematical terms this is given as:

i.e. $\sigma = \sqrt{\Sigma (x - \bar{x})^2 / n}$

A low standard deviation indicates that the values tend to be close to the mean, while a high standard deviation indicates that the values are spread out over a wider range giving an idea of how diverse a class may be for a particular test instrument or aggregated results. This may make sense to some parents or employers.

Other teachers may even take this further and attempt to use **Z-scores** (Standard Scores). A standard score is the number of standard deviations by which the value of a raw score (i.e., the student's score) is above or below the mean of that test instrument or total score. Raw scores above the mean have <u>positive</u> standard scores, while those below the mean have <u>negative</u> standard scores.

Z-scores are calculated by subtracting the class mean from the individual's raw score and then dividing the difference by the standard deviation for that class.

$$\text{i.e. } \textbf{z-score} = \frac{(x - \bar{x})}{\sigma}$$

Z-scores are useful if there are a number of test instrument of different standards (or even in different classes) which need to be compared. It also gives the student's position in terms of how far they are away from the mean in the given population. But be careful! Few students, school administrators and parents are interested in complex statistical analyses!

More on z-scores at:

http://www2.econ.iastate.edu/classes/crp274/swenson/CRP272/What%20is%20a%20Z%20score.pdf

https://www.discoveringstatistics.com/docs/zscores.pdf

https://www.wsfcs.k12.nc.us/cms/lib/NC01001395/Centricity/Domain/3165/calculating_z_scores.pdf

If the teacher feels that these standard scores should be expressed as a percentage so that parents can understand them, then z-scores can be converted by:

https://measuringu.com/pcalcz/

Well, statistics can be rather tiresome to calculate for several classes of students and the statistics may be useful for the institution but also confusing for parents who are not into statistics. It is NOT a smart idea to use statistics to impress or bamboozle students and parents. Keep the maths simple and in terms which can be simply communicated.

Assessment of students is about giving them and other stakeholders (mainly parents) some idea (good or bad) as to how the student is performing. Unfortunately, some of a teacher's role at parent nights or at private interviews is the interpretation of statistics or how grades have been achieved. It is always useful to begin by giving an honest, verbal evaluation in simple terms.

Chapter 9

How, When & Why…
More on Learning Theories

9.1 So why bother?

During teacher training years or doing post-graduate degrees, one is exposed (rightly so) to a number of theories of learning. Like any theory, these are subject to change as research into education and learning unearths new truths about how people learn.

Educational research can be fascinating, not to mention just plain hard work, but like all research it usually becomes an obsession with the researcher. Once there is an interest, and good research questions are generated, the search for a valid research methodology is finally found and then its application becomes very much like an absorbing detective investigation. Usually, the research generates more questions than answers to the original questions previously posed. The place for such excitement is in a university which offers research facilities (and hopefully scholarships!).

A detailed discussion on learning theory was not going to be part of this basic survival book, but some knowledge of the main theories would be very good for understanding of how to teach and everyday classroom application. A useful site about educational theories can be found at:

https://www.aussieeducator.org.au/education/theo ries.html

9.2 Then there are themes

The classroom teacher, and to some extent the corporate instructor, is often subject to additional themes or programs which their corporate or political masters wish to introduce; usually for their concept about the 'good of the community'.

Government ministers (and corporate CEO's) often get a sudden flash of activity which leads them on to have their minions develop 'social programs' which of course, will be taught in schools or the company; usually as an addendum to the already over-crowded curriculum or daily tasks.

Sometimes these new programs are based upon an apparent perception of community needs and it is not uncommon for these to be developed as a result of some authoritative pressure. The Media or the Government will demand that teachers take on these new programs and educate the young over and above what is already being taught.

A series of dreadful car accidents? Let's have a 'safe driving' course. A sudden spate of swimming pool drownings? Let's have a 'learn to swim' campaign.

Over my career, I have had to either teach such programs as additional learning sessions or integrate the new 'philosophies' within existing teaching programs. Most of these are very valuable to the students and their community so teachers usually get very much involved. These have included:

- learn to swim (often in summer months as weeks taken out of class time);

- outdoor education programs and cadet courses (holiday time);

- cultural and language appreciation. Sometimes these become 'emersion' courses which are taught in class time in all subjects;

- First Nation or indigenous emersion;

- multi-cultural perspectives;

- the 3Rs (Reading, wRiting and aRithmetic are often re-invented as an immediate social concern that the current generation is illiterate and maths-challenged);

- drugs and alcohol programs;

- driver safety and road rules;

- gender equity is often written into syllabuses as mandatory perspectives but sometimes become special programs; and

- interfaith programs. Just to name a few.

One year the State Minister of Education, a keen snow skier was determined that every student should learn how to ski. Australia has some good snowfields in the high south east country, but it was a bit difficult to explain why students in the flat, far regions of desert country two thousand kilometres away, needed to know how to ski, especially when they had never seen snow! Well, at least the in-service courses at a swank ski resort were fun for teachers who participated! (Yay, me!)

Regardless of the introduction of such programs, teachers need to be flexible and use whatever learning theories possible to get on with the job of instructing their students as best they can.

9.3 Are learning theories useful in the classroom?

Yes, as they are useful to give teachers some background about what researchers have found out about how people learn. Teachers can then create specific strategies and techniques to apply these learning theories in their classroom to make maximum use of their own talents in the art of communication.

An understanding of learning theories helps teachers connect to the many different personalities of students within their classroom. Teachers can focus on different learning styles to reach different students, creating teaching that focuses directly on student needs and aptitudes.

There are many paradigms of learning theory, but the most commonly expressed and used paradigms include:

- behaviourism;
- cognitivism;
- constructivism;
- humanism; and
- connectivism.

9.4 Behaviourism

Behaviourism as a theory was first established by John B. Watson (American Psychologist: 1878-1958) who believed that all Human behaviours are the result of experience and that any person can be trained to act in a particular manner given the right conditioning.

So, in general terms, Behaviourism is based on the idea that all behaviours are learned through a response to external stimuli and a corresponding change or conditioning. Ivan Pavlov (Russian

Physiologist: 1849-1936) conditioned dogs to salivate on hearing a bell which was associated with the previous act of giving food. This concept of classical conditioning then was generalised to the Human practice of learning.

Edward Thorndike (American Psychologist: 1874-1948) suggested that his Law of Effect could control conditioning through reinforcement (positive or negative) until the repeated use of the stimulus produced new associations and thus learning occurs.

B.F. Skinner (American Psychologist: 1904-1990) thought that such classical conditioning was too simple a model to explain some aspects of learning, especially those areas which were of natural interest to the student rather than simple physiological needs. He proposed that these and similar behaviours, called *operants*, would be learnt if they were presented as stimuli and then reinforced by adding a reward or removing a punishment; the former being preferred in the classroom.

In the classroom, a teacher can 'condition' (NOT 'brain-wash') their students to respond to certain stimuli such as raising a raising a hand to get silence (beats yelling!) or encouraging students to answer questions by the promise of a reward. This may range from a simple verbal encouragement to some more practical treat as a jelly bean (or some healthier treat!). The use of rewards and punishment in schools has long been used to modify student behaviour and foster harder, more productive work. Continued punishments usually resulted in a dislike for a teacher, subject or education in general. In more recent years, the harsh Draconian punishments of the past have thankfully given way to more humane rewards or at worse some form of mild exclusion.

9.5 Cognitivism

The Cognitive Theory sees the student as an information processor and tries find out how this is done through the processes of perception, attention, language, memory, thinking, and consciousness.

This approach assumes that internal mental processes occurs between the input of stimuli, from the teacher for example, and response or output shown as a result of this learning.

Cognitive processing can be affected by the mental framework of beliefs and expectations developed within the student from experience. These were called *schemas* and as one got older, these became more detailed and sophisticated. These would help students to organise and interpret new information quickly and effectively, and prevent the student from being overwhelmed by the vast amount of information perceived in their environment.

Noam Chomsky (American linguist and philosopher: 1928 -   ) believed that the processes of language was an innate ability of all children rather than a result of simple behavioural conditioning. This innate ability would allow children to develop further patterns of grammar and other forms of learning.

When adopting a cognitivist approach to classroom teaching, the teacher should consider the student is an active participant in the learning process who will use various strategies to process and construct their personal understanding of the lesson content. The role of teachers should be to present ideal conditions under which the material can be learnt rather than explicitly giving it to the students. Activities which would promote cognitive learning would include those which promote creativity, interaction, discovery and problem solving through the use of creative language.

9.6 Constructivism

Constructivism sees learning as an active process with the student actively building or creating their own subjective representations of objective reality. New information is linked to and builds upon or modifies prior personal knowledge. That is, each individual has a distinctive point of view, based on existing knowledge and values and so within the one lesson, teaching or activity may result in different learning by each pupil, as their subjective interpretations differ.

Jean Piaget (Swiss Psychologist: 1896 – 1980) and Jerome Brunner (American Psychologist: 1915-2016) both supported a cognitive constructivism approach to learning which stated that knowledge is actively constructed by learners based on their existing cognitive structures and is relative to their stage of cognitive development.

Jean **Piaget**'s theory suggests that intelligence changes as children grow and that they have to develop or construct a mental model of the world through time. Their development occurs through the interaction of innate capacities and environmental events, and they pass through a series of stages:

- **Sensorimotor stage**: birth to 18-24 months – in which the child experiences the world through its senses from an egocentric point of view through coordinating sensory experiences (seeing, hearing) with motor actions (reaching, touching). Development is very rapid with the child beginning to explore new experiences and objects with a growth in symbolic thinking.

- **Preoperational stage**: 2 to 7 years – now their self-involvement begins to weaken and they begin to perceive the world from the perspectives of others as well as their own. New motor skills develop but as yet logical thinking is weak;
- **Concrete operational stage: 7 to 11 years** – is when children begin to think rationally and logically but only in very simple, concrete

terms and often with the use of aids. They begin to think in terms of object features such as number, area, volume, orientation as well as concepts of reversibility, sequence and to recognize relationships among various things in a serial order. The also begin to see the perspectives of others now class inclusion becomes important; and the

- **Formal operational stage**: after age 11 – independent thinking is beginning to develop and they can do mathematical calculations, think creatively, use abstract reasoning, and imagine the outcome of particular actions.

Jerome Brunner contributed much to the theory of cognitive constructivism by promoting the concept of discovery learning. This was to be achieved by the method of inquiry-based instruction in which students were to discover facts and relationships for themselves.

New problem-solving situations then, required students to draw upon their own past experiences and existing knowledge to discover new facts, relationships and truths. Students interact with the world by exploring and manipulating objects, being critical about questions and controversies and performing experiments.

By self-inquiry and experimentation, students were more likely to remember concepts and knowledge discovered on their own in contrast to simply being presented with facts and ideas. Brunner's work is compatible with that of Jean Piaget in that students must be able to reach that stage of development where they can independently think and experiment.

Another proponent of constructivism was **Lev Vygotsky** (Russian Psychologist: 1896-1934) who believed that constructive learning was socially driven. His Sociocultural Theory suggests that children acquire their cultural values, beliefs, and problem-solving strategies through collaborative dialogues within and between communities, especially with the more knowledgeable members of the society.

Unlike Piaget's idea that the child's development must precede their learning, Vygotsky argued that learning is a necessary aspect of the process of development and that social learning tends to come before development.

A more recent view of constructivism is that Radical Constructivism of **Ernst von Glasersfeld** (German Philosopher and Psychologist: 1917 -2010). Radical constructivism suggests that learning is based on one's own experience and interpretation rather than that taught by teachers. Thus, the individual constructs knowledge, understanding and links this with their own experiences and ideas and so learns.

So, putting all of this together, the responsibility of the teacher is to create a collaborative problem-solving environment where students become active participants in their own learning. That is, the teacher acts as a facilitator of learning rather than an instructor.

To do this effectively so that students will construct their own learning, it is important for teachers to know of the abilities, strengths and weaknesses and the intellectual level of their students. Teacher may have to use *scaffolding* within their lessons, that is where they continually adjust the level of their assistance in response to the learner's level of performance.

9.5 Humanism

Humanism theory concentrates on the individual and asserts that learning is a natural process that helps a person reach complete realization of their potential and abilities. Finding new experiences, exploring and observing others and role modelling are important factors in humanistic learning.

Abraham Maslow (American Psychologist: 1908 – 1970) suggested that there was a 'Hierarchy of Needs' in which a person must sequentially acquire before reaching self-actualisation. These can be summarised in the following chart:

HIGH	NEEDS	FEATURES	TYPE
	Self-actualization	morality, creativity, problem solving. Lack of prejudice	Self-fulfillment Needs
	Esteem Needs	confidence, self-esteem, achievement, respect	Psychological Needs
	Belongingness & Love Needs	love, friendship, intimacy, family	
	Safety Needs	security of environment, employment, resources, health, property	Basic Needs
LOW	Physiological Needs	Basic needs of air, food, water, sex, sleep, homeostasis (same state of body functions)	

Figure Table 9.1: Maslow's Hierarchy of Needs

In the classroom, the relationship between the teacher and the student is most important. The teacher is responsible for creating an environment where the basic and psychological needs are met. The teacher should be sincere, be able to express understanding and care for the students as well as respecting their emotions and appreciate their potential and needs. To achieve such a healthy classroom environment, the teacher should also have a firm but friendly way of ensuring that students' freedom is extended to all without interference to self-control.

9.7 Connectivism

This is based upon the idea that people process information by forming connections. Such theory is promoted by **George Siemens** (American Educator: 1970 -) and **Stephen Downes** (Canadian Philosopher: 1959 -). It suggests that people no longer stop learning after formal education and continue to gain knowledge from other avenues such as job skills, networking, experience and access to information with new tools in technology. It is very much entrenched in the example of commuter networks and group connections.

Knowledge is constantly changing and in networks is not controlled or created by any formal organization but tends to be chaotic; shifting as information flows across networks that themselves are inter-connected with other networks.

Learning in the classroom can take place as a student-centred group activity where each student contributes some information to the others. It may involve the use of blogs on various Internet sites and discussions with other networked groups on particular topics. Learning then becomes a very fluid and self-motivated activity.

For more information on this theory see:

https://www.youtube.com/watch?v=yx5VHpaW8s
Q (Dr George Siemens on Connectivism)

https://www.downes.ca/post/38653
(Dr. *Stephen Downes* on Connectivism)

9.8 Learning for the 21st Century

Modern researchers and teachers who are keen on research usually adopt a futurist approach. That is, they try to adapt teaching to meet the rapid changes which are constantly evolving within society.

Without straying too far from the more traditional necessities of the 3Rs, educators are now becoming aware of the need for new attributes of learning such as:

- critical thinking and problem-solving;

- collaboration;

- creativity and innovation;

- cross-cultural and gender understanding;

- communication;

- computing technology; and

- career learning.

It would be difficult within a modern school to totally ignore the effects and influences of computers, the Internet and social media platforms upon students. These can be used within the classroom but also their influence outside needs to be recognised as there are many bad influences as well useful ones. Handling social media is becoming a major concern amongst educators who find that they have to control its use within the classroom as well as supporting students and their parents against some of the harmful effects such as cyber-bullying.

In some schools, the 21st century has yet to arrive and so there is little concern about the use of modern technology within the classroom, but the outside problems, frustrations and aspirations of students using mobile phones and various forms of social interaction still remain.

Moreover, the use of the Internet and global news services have brought students into a world with considerable problems which they will inherit. Environmental change and global warming, racial and religious persecution, international conflicts, economic uncertainty and jobs are just a few barriers which students may see as having to be overcome as they grow into adulthood and have to deal with these uncertainties. Educators cannot simply revert to acceptable traditional curricula and ignore what is affecting the wider society outside of the school.

The problem here is that teachers now have to have some idea of the students' concerns and be able to assist them with these matters as well as teaching some of the core values still necessary in learning. Teachers will also have these concerns and may have difficulty in providing some of the answers or strategies needed to alleviate anxiety or to assist in making the future world a better place.

In the past, educational authorities were notorious in suddenly introducing various themes into teaching as an additional task or as an 'enrichment' program. These themes often came about as a 'knee-jerk' reaction to some political perception of a particular social issue. For example, if the number of racially-motivated crimes increased then there most likely would be an introduced program of racial harmony. Often this would be seen by all as an 'add-on' function of learning rather than a true need which should be reflected by all of society.

Changes in teaching about social responsibility needs to be integrated as part of the normal school curricula as well as from media outlets and other social communication systems so that it becomes part of a larger movement towards change. Single-issue needs may be put down as rants from the usual 'rent-a-crowd' protesters and may not be taken seriously, however they may spark some awareness of the need to address such problems, especially within a well-planned and responsible curriculum. Some reasons for adopting a futures perspective within a classroom are given in the table below:

Needs	Reasons
Critical Thinking	A great influx of opinion and information will require the student to think carefully about issues and to be able to have an informed opinion.
Clarifying Values	With such increase in opinion, students will need to be able to clearly understand the meaning of each
Decision Making	Identifications of important values will require the best choices to be made
Creative Imagination	Rapid changes in society and the environment will require solutions based on innovation
Responsibility of Action	Global interaction requires the future citizen to be responsible for their actions and to participate in social cooperation

Table 9.2 Need for a futures perspective.

There will need to be considerable change within schools by the current and next generation of teachers to meet the needs of future generations. Some useful resources may be found at:

https://files.eric.ed.gov/fulltext/ED603249.pdf

https://nsuworks.nova.edu/cgi/viewcontent.cgi?article=1014&context=innovate

https://www.oecd.org/site/educeri21st/40756908.pdf
https://easdinnovativelearning.weebly.com/uploads/7/7/1/6/77162025/p21_framework_definitions_new_logo_2015.pdf

https://www.imls.gov/assets/1/AssetManager/Bishop%20Pre-Con%202.pdf

https://remakelearning.org/blog/2016/04/29/demystifying-learning-frameworks-the-p21-framework/

https://www.amazon.com/Surviving-Global-Warming-Guide-Future-ebook/dp/B0868F7FDK/ref=sr_1_1?dchild=1&keyw

ords=surviving+global+warming+Peter+T+Scott&qi
d=1609192988&sr=8-1

9.9 DIY learning research

Teachers usually have close contact with their
students and often perceive their needs and how
they affect the wider education system. It is no
wonder then, that many teachers take on research,
sometimes internally, within their own classroom
such as doing a simple socio-metric analysis of who
likes who or some simple survey of likes and
dislikes. If it could be a major issue (and it will get
back to the parents and then the Principal), then
official sanction from both the school authorities and
the parents will be require.

Most often, the teacher may embark on the arduous
but rewarding task of doing some formal research as
part of post-graduate studies at a college or
university. Having done all of my university courses
(one Bachelor's Degree, two Masters and one
Doctorate) part-time, after school whilst
participating in school extra-curricula activities,
having a family and some sort of private life, isn't

easy. Many teacher post-graduate students find that the time and tasks required are just too much and drop out. I was simply stubborn, motivated by the 'you can't do that!' challenge and did not get much sleep. But my researches were fascinating and given very positive reviews regarding making a valuable contribution to such research. Perhaps the reader may find something useful from my example.

Having spent seven years part time completing my Bachelors' Degree in Science with a major in Geology with sub-majors in Chemistry and Psychology, I now felt that I could psychoanalyse rocks very effectively but it helped in my teaching. It also slowed down my social life (a little) and I vowed never to set foot inside a university again.

As fate moves in unexpected ways, I ended up doing more studies, initially reluctantly and then one gets immersed into the research and finds that the pursuit of the answers to the research questions becomes an obsession. It is somewhat like becoming Sherlock Holmes and being an active participant in one of his most complicated cases.

My Master's Degree in Geology consisted of pure research and the five-year exploration and mapping of 800 square kilometres of rugged country. Great exercise and useful later as an example for my future Earth Science students. Later I took on a Masters of Educational Administration which had been denied to me earlier. It was four-year correspondence program of coursework (communications, economics, law, research methods) and a thesis in communications within schools. A very interesting program which I did in two-years ('you can't do that!'). It taught me that in the typical large Secondary school:

- communication is best done directly face to face;

- use of the telephone is the next best thing, especially with parents;

- emails can be difficult, especially if one gets about 50 each day and is expected to answer them (before school);

- school secretaries (especially of the Senior Administration) often filter out communication, acting as 'gate-keepers' and passing on only what they think the recipient needs (so the personal touch is needed);

- noticeboards with staff messages are often unread; and

- the 'grape-vine' system of communications within the student body is the most effective way of both learning what is going on and transmitting important messages;

A very useful piece of research in being able to communicate in schools and the economics/law sections were useful in persuading the Administration that they should provide more support to teachers.

The Doctorate was a full-on, part-time program at a university which wanted to introduce post-graduate research. It was full research with no course work (lectures) other than some seminars. It was a 'professional degree' that is, aimed at the education profession so that candidates had to have a minimum of five years teaching experience before even applying. About 50 applied, eight were selected and one graduated four years later.

My research was another case study in a large, well-established and prestigious private school. I was lucky enough to be given the support of the Principal, fellow staff members as well as the students, parents and ex-students association. The aims were to find out what features made up the school's culture and how they were communicated to the wider community.

My methodology included a sensitizing survey of general, open-ended questions about the school which led to the construction of a more extensive survey using a Likert-scale of 1 to 5 for each question. These were about aspects of the school's culture discovered in the first survey. Some additional depth was provided through interviews from members of the school's community and observation of how the school generally operated.

This last technique was from the point of view of 'an inside observer' i.e., someone who was part of the system and could therefore move freely through it making detailed observations. This was very much like that which would be used by an accepted anthropologist and indeed, a school student body could be considered as 'tribal'. Unlike some of the famous anthropologists, I had been already accepted into the tribe and had a senior position of trust; somewhere between some sort of 'witchdoctor', and local pirate chief. I occasionally set fire to the school through science experiment, made various astronomical predictions from my observatory; (about rain on 'astronomy nights' and always incorrect) and ran the school's Naval Cadet unit along Viking lines (the school's theme).

I found that a school's culture is the overall identity of the school; how its people in all of the 'clans' (staff, students, parents, ex-students) interacted with each other and shared common values. A strong school culture is important to the good health and happiness of all of its people; a most important factor in teaching.

Shared values were both tangible and intangible and all were very important to the school's 'clans'. The tangible values concerned those of the appearance of the school, its uniforms and of the symbols of the school which had high, almost spiritual meaning.

The intangible values of the school were less apparent but extremely important as they set the standards for behaviour, personal performance and allegiance to the school. These were <u>what the school was about and which set it apart from other schools</u>.

Tangible elements of the school's culture included the appearance of the school itself; a red brick, mock gothic set of buildings with the standard colonnade quadrangle and tiled rooves. Lawns, trees, gardens and playing fields made up the rest of this aspect of the school's culture. An attempt by the school's administration to build new buildings which departed from this model met with stiff opposition from most factions and a redesign of the future construction.

The student uniforms, school badge and motto were also important identifiers of the tribe. Apart from the very few untidy types who did not maintain their uniform, everyone strived to look professional. Staff also followed this line and heaven help (it <u>is</u> a church school!) the slob teacher who arrived in jeans! The attitude here was that students were being taught to become professionals and other proud members of a responsible society so standards should be maintained. There was never any view that such dress standards infringed on individual freedom as the uniformity of the system made everyone 'equal' within the tribe and so they could have their freedom in more important matters.

Intangible values were harder to discover but it was gratifying to find a correlation of various attitudes amongst all of the clans. Striving for excellence, helping each other and being generally an all-round person both in sport, study and the many other school activities were the most important shared values of the school.

Not having any precedents of such research in schools meant that I had to look at the culture of corporations. Organisational culture was apparently a big thing in the world of business where the communication of the company's beliefs and standards were important to attract customers. Similar aspects were found within my target school and like many successful corporations who had high values and meaningful logos which identified both the company and its underlying values, the school was very successful.

The corporate or school culture usually was set up by the founder who had a long-term vision for the organisation. In my school this was well planned and set up over the first few years by the founder. It was also then strengthened by his chosen successor who saw the importance of such culture and it had been maintained ever since.

One important and unexpected finding was that in modern times, the values of the school were mostly passed on by the senior students, especially the boarders who held strongly to the founder's aspiration. The Principal and staff maintained the school's culture but the senior students were its guardians who then transmitted these values to the new students as they arrived.

There were some underlying values which were the prerogative of the students which were known to ex-students and a few trusted staff such as myself. Ways of behaving (all appropriate of course!), how to wear the uniform (the hats especially were to be worn in a casual manner) and secret codes for gently chiding non-conformists were passed on in great secrecy.

For teachers coming into a school with a strong culture, fitting in and having a good relationship with the students and other members of staff meant becoming immersed in and supporting this culture.

Unfortunately, some schools develop in a haphazard way and so have little or no culture, or one which is thoroughly toxic, which operate on the principle of 'survival of the fittest'. I have taught in some of these schools and the best advice for new teachers is to try and make some improvement by introducing some enrichment such as sporting, cultural activity or community assistance program.

It can be done but it requires effort and cooperation between the entire staff and parents. If this is not possible, then the teacher can only do the best they can within their own classroom. This is easier to do but still takes a lot of hard work only after one has gained the confidence of the class by being firm, fair and trying to understand the problems of each student.

So, there is still much to look into as far as learning research is concerned. The common feature that those who do research is that it opens up many more questions than answers. The future holds a lot of new challenges and it is apparent that there are many major concerns which confront the student of the future. Global warming, pandemics, economic instability, gender/racial/religious abuse and poverty just to name a few to frighten the future citizens of this world. However, a long period of teaching also shows one the resilience and adaptability of the younger generation and so I personally am very optimistic about a marvellous future and see innovative and effective education as the operant of change.

Remember, a good teacher is also a good learner.

If you want a cure for insomnia, then my Doctoral Thesis can be found at:

https://acuresearchbank.acu.edu.au/download/6f70f4c53
3aee5a029abec18fa02833add0e6d0dff8e96f7d44bea5c5c6
cd7f4/19219100/65077_downloaded_stream_302.pdf

Have a great career!

References

Anderson, L.W. (Ed.), *et al.*, (2001). *A taxonomy for learning, teaching, and assessing: A revision of Bloom's Taxonomy of Educational Objectives*. New York: Longman.

Aubrey, K. and Riley, R. (2018) *Understanding and Using Educational Theories*. London SAGE.

Aussie Educator, (2020). *Learning Theories*. (an alphabetical list of major learning theories and researchers).https://www.aussieeducator.org.au/education/theories.html

Bloom, B. S.; Engelhart, M. D.; Furst, E. J.; Hill, W. H.; *Krathwohl*, D. R. (1956). *Taxonomy of educational objectives: The classification of educational goals. Handbook I: Cognitive domain. New York: David McKay Company.*

Cherry, K. (2019). Gardner's Theory of Multiple Intelligences. Verywellmind, July 17, 2017. https://www.verywellmind.com/gardners-theory-of-multiple-intelligences-2795161

Davis, K., Christodoulou, J., Seider, S., Gardner, H. (2011), *The Theory of Multiple Intelligences"*, in Sternberg, R. J. and Kaufman, B. *(Eds.), The Cambridge Handbook of Intelligence, Cambridge University Press, pp. 485–503.*

Ertmer, P. A. and Newby, T. J. (2013). *Behaviorism, cognitivism, constructivism: Comparing critical features from an instructional design perspective.* Performance Improvement Quarterly, 26(2), 43-71.

Gardner, H. (2011). *Frames of mind: The theory of multiple intelligences.* Hachette United Kingdom.

Illeris, K. (Edit.) (2018). *Contemporary Theories of Learning - Learning Theorists ... In Their Own Words.* Abingdon (UK): Routledge.276 Pages.

Krathwohl, D.R., Bloom, B.S., & Masia, B.B. (1964). *Taxonomy of educational objectives, the classification of educational goals, handbook II: Affective domain.* New York: David McKay Co., Inc.

Maslow, A. H. (2013). *Toward a psychology of being.* Start Publishing LLC.

McLeod, S. A. (5 Feb., 2017). *Behaviorist approach.* Simply Psychology.
https://www.simplypsychology.org/behaviorism.html

Newton, P. M., Da Silva, A., Peters, L. G. (2020). *A pragmatic master list of action verbs for Bloom's taxonomy.* Frontiers in Education. *5*. 10 July, 2020.

Scott, P.T. (1976). (with G. Comino). *Junior Science Teaching.* University of New England, Armidale, external notes for Diploma of Education program.

Scott, P.T. (1976). (with G. Comino). *Senior Science Teaching.* University of New England, Armidale, external notes for Diploma of Education program.

Scott, P.T. (1977). (with G. Comino) *Teaching Science to the Slow-learner.* Upsurge. 32. NSW Dept. Education. Sydney; pp6-10.

Scott, P.T., (1977). *Pupil Variables and Teacher Interaction.* Inside Education, 71(3). NSW Dept. Education, Sydney; pp.15-20.

Scott, P.T. (1978). *Designing Unit Programs for Junior Science.* Science & Ag. Bull. 1 (3) NW Region, NSW Dept. Ed., Tamworth; pp3-21

Scott, P.T. (1980). (with J. Pow & F. Tebbutt). *Curriculum Ideas for the Implementation of the Science Syllabus. Years 11 & 12 Two Unit Geology.* NSW Education Department, Sydney. 48 pages.

Scott, P.T. (1984). *Sketching Skills for Science Staff.* Science & Ag. Bull. 6 (3) NW Region, NSW Dept. Ed., Tamworth; pp32-44.

Scott, P.T. (1984). *Psychology – the Science of the Mind.* NSW Government Printer, Sydney, 83 pages.

Scott, P.T. (1992). *Communications in the Large Private School.* University of New England, M.Ed.Admin. Thesis (unpublished). 151 pages.

Scott, P.T. (1992). (Chairman/Editor) *Senior Syllabus in Earth Science.* Board of Senior Secondary Schools Studies, Queensland Government.

Scott, P.T. (1999). *Communications of School Culture.* Australian Catholic University, Brisbane, Ed.D. Thesis (unpublished). 315 pages.

Shabatura, J. (2013) Using Bloom's Taxonomy to Write Effective Learning Objectives. Assignments & Measuring Student Learning, University of Arkansas. Sept 27, 2013:https://tips.uark.edu/using-blooms-taxonomy/

Skinner, B. F. (1976). *About Behaviorism.* New York: Vintage Books.

Stevens-Fulbrook, P. (2020). *15 Learning Theories in Education (A Complete Summary).* Teacher of Sci.com (UK). https://teacherofsci.com/learning-theories-in-education/

Vygotsky, L. S. (1978 *Mind in society: the development of higher psychological processes. Chapter 6.* Cambridge, Massachusetts: Harvard University Press. pp. 79–91.

For those teachers thinking about retirement and/or have concerns about their finances, see:

Scott, W.J. (2016*). Debt Free: The Morals of Money Management.* Brisbane, Felix Publications.

About the Author

Dr. Scott at his staffroom desk

Dr. Peter Terence Scott was born in Sydney, Australia and had a professional teaching career spanning over forty years. He was educated at Maroubra Junction Primary School and Randwick Boys' High School. A graduate of a condensed, two-year program in Junior Secondary Teaching at Sydney Teachers' College, he began his teaching career at age 19 as Acting Head of Science at a new school in Canberra, Australia's capital. He has taught in a number of schools, both State and Private, and studied part-time at university, obtaining a Bachelor of Science degree, Masters' Degrees in Science and Educational Administration and later a Doctorate in Education. For many years he was the Head of the State Syllabus Committee in his subject area and Member of the State Advisory Council in Science Teaching and the State Committee which teaching monitored and awarded the final Senior Certificates. He was also a member of several industry committees, an Army Reserve Officer and an Officer/Instructor in the Australian Naval Cadets. Now retired, he lives in Brisbane, Australia.

Other Books by the Author

FICTION

Letters from San Rafael (as Hernan Moreno Ruiz). Set in South America in the 1880's, this is a collection of letters smuggled home by Don Hernan Moreno, an Intelligence officer of the Peruvian Army who has been captured by the Ecuadorans during a border dispute. Taken to the fortified hacienda in Banos, in the mountains of Ecudor, he and his sargeant, Garcia, are treated as honoured guests. Each of the ten stories tells of the life and times of people in the hacienda and beyond. The final chapter is the climax of the entire book.

Return to San Rafael is the sequel to LETTERS from SAN RAFAEL. It is now 1891 and it has been five years since Colonel Moreno and his faithful sergeant Garcia had escaped San Rafael. Now, Moreno receives a mysterious coded letter asking them to return to San Rafael to solve its secret and ensure the stability of both Ecuador and Peru.

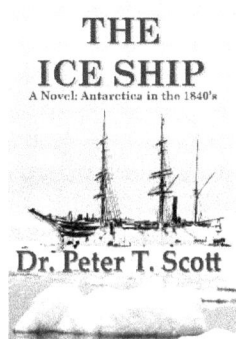

The Ice Ship. Set mainly in the Antarctic in the 1840's, this is the story of the survival of the crew of the futuristic auxiliary steam whaler, the *AUSTRALIS* which has become trapped in the ice following its voyage south along the Antarctic Peninsula. Based upon actual observations and experience of the author during a 2011 voyage into the same region on a small ex-research vessel.

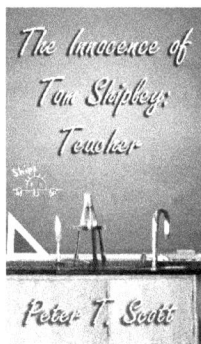

The Innocence of Tom Shipley is the first novel about young teacher Tom Shipley. It begins during his days at High School and his penchant as a Laboratory Prefect in making explosives and other prankish devices, follows him through similar acts at Teachers College and then out into his first appointment at age nineteen into the profession of teaching. At a brand-new school in Canberra, he finds that as the sole Science teacher, he is now the Acting Head of Department charged with establishing this subject at the school and equipping and managing several laboratories and new incoming staff. **A 'must read' for all teachers and parents.**

Tom Shipley's War is a sequel to the INNOCENCE of TOM SHIPLEY and is about the young man's protest against those who protested about National Servicemen who were called up for the Vietnam War. He volunteers for the local Citizens' Military Forces unit (later the Army Reserve) and finds another war entirely: one with the more conservative members of the Army who still believe in WW2 tactics. Based on the author's own experiences as a young officer.

NON-FICTION

Adventures in Earth Science is an in-depth, traditional Earth Science textbook on Geology, Meteorology, Oceanography and Astronomy. The latest scientific information has been given in the text including chapters on climate change and the future use of fuels and energy. The book contains over 700 pages, 1200 photographs and illustrations mostly taken by the author. It also includes 32 video links taken by the author to explain various skills as well as excursions to many exotic places in support of the text. Also has companion **Teachers' Guide** and **Laboratory Manual**.

The contents of this book have also been rearranged into the **Adventures in Earth Science Series** of eight smaller individual books in both electronic and A5 print editions.

| Exploration Science | Fossils- Life in the Rocks | Riches from the Earth | A Dangerous Planet: Volcanoes & Earthquakes |

| Rocks - Building The Earth | Changing the Surface: Weathering & Erosion | Through Sea & Sky: Oceanography/ meteorology | Beyond Planet Earth: Astronomy |

Adventures in Earth and Environmental Science is a two-volume textbook on the environment, how it is monitored and implications for the future. They come in electronic format and as A4-sized print editions with a **Laboratory Manual** for each volume and a **Teachers' Guide**.

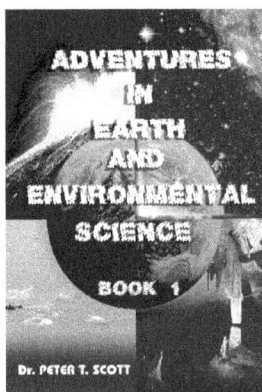

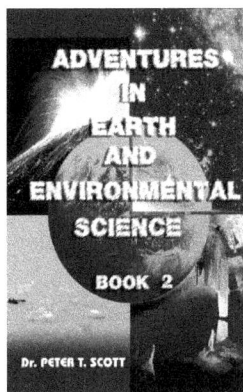

Surviving Global Warming - A Guide for the Future is a comprehensive explanation of the natural and man-made causes of global warming with data from a wide range of reputable scientific bodies such as CSIRO and NASA. Written with many innovative suggestions for coping with the consequences of future global warming at the home, local and government levels. It comes as an electronic or printed edition.

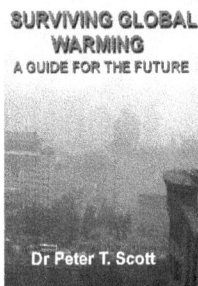

A Pocketbook for Hiking and Survival is a concise reference book on going into the wild places of the Earth based on the author's extensive experience as a hiker, caver, geologist, Infantry Officer, ski instructor and leader of several youth groups. Topics include basic equipment, food, water, shelter, rope work, navigation and communications. The book is designed to be carried in pocket or backpack to where mobile phone signals may be lost. It is available in Kindle format as well as paperback and it is recommended that mobile phone users install it as a stand-alone document.

A Pocketbook for
Hiking and Survival

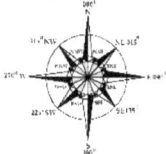

Dr Peter T. Scott

All of these books are available in electronic format for any PC or tablet in Kindle format which can be read on any device using the free Kindle App. Or as print editions. Available at all Internet book outlets or from **Felix Publishing** by contacting them at:

info.felixpublishing@gmail.com

www.ingramcontent.com/pod-product-compliance
Lightning Source LLC
Chambersburg PA
CBHW062117020426
42335CB00013B/997